Houghton Mifflin Reading
Tennessee

D1517875

Teacher's Edition

Kindergarten

Colors All Around

Senior Authors J. David Cooper, John J. Pikulski

Authors David J. Chard, Gilbert G. Garcia, Claude N. Goldenberg, Phyllis C. Hunter, Marjorie Y. Lipson, Shane Templeton, Sheila W. Valencia, MaryEllen Vogt

Consultants Linda H. Butler, Linnea C. Ehri, Carla B. Ford

HOUGHTON MIFFLIN

BOSTON

TENNESSEE REVIEWERS

Maryellen Eaves, Cordova, Tennessee; **Tim Hamilton,** Metro/Nashville Public Schools, Tennessee; **Vicki Haney,** Metro/Nashville Public Schools, Tennessee; **Fran Hewston Gregory,** Metro/Nashville Public Schools, Tennessee; **Deborah L. Smith,** Metro/Nashville Public Schools, Tennessee; **Linda L. Wyatt,** Metro/Nashville Public Schools, Tennessee

LITERATURE REVIEWERS

Consultants: Dr. Adela Artola Allen, Associate Dean, Graduate College, Associate Vice President for Inter-American Relations, University of Arizona, Tucson, AZ; **Dr. Manley Begay,** Co-director of the Harvard Project on American Indian Economic Development, Director of the National Executive Education Program for Native Americans, Harvard University, John F. Kennedy School of Government, Cambridge, MA; **Dr. Nicholas Kannellos,** Director, Arte Publico Press, Director, Recovering the U.S. Hispanic Literacy Heritage Project, University of Houston, TX; **Mildred Lee,** author and former head of Library Services for Sonoma County, Santa Rosa, CA; **Dr. Barbara Moy,** Director of the Office of Communication Arts, Detroit Public Schools, MI; **Norma Naranjo,** Clark County School District, Las Vegas, NV; **Dr. Arlette Ingram Willis,** Associate Professor, Department of Curriculum and Instruction, Division of Language and Literacy, University of Illinois at Urbana-Champaign, IL

Teachers: Helen Brooks, Vestavia Hills Elementary School, Birmingham, Alabama; **Patricia Buchanan,** Thurgood Marshall School, Newark, Delaware; **Gail Connor,** Language Arts Resource Teacher, Duval County, Jacksonville, Florida; **Vicki DeMott,** McLean Science/Technology School, Wichita, Kansas; **Marge Egenhoffer,** Dixon Elementary School, Brookline, Wisconsin; **Mary Jew Mori,** Griffin Avenue Elementary, Los Angeles, California

PROGRAM REVIEWERS

Linda Bayer, Jonesboro, GA; **Sheri Blair,** Warner Robins, GA; **Faye Blake,** Jacksonville, FL; **Suzi Boyett,** Sarasota, FL; **Carol Brockhouse,** Madison Schools, Wayne Westland Schools, MI; **Patti Brustad,** Sarasota, FL; **Jan Buckelew,** Venice, FL; **Maureen Carlton,** Barstow, CA; **Karen Cedar,** Gold River, CA; **Karen Ciraulo,** Folsom, CA; **Marcia M. Clark,** Griffin, GA; **Kim S. Coady,** Covington, GA; **Eva Jean Conway,** Valley View School District, IL; **Marilyn Crownover,** Tustin, CA; **Carol Daley,** Sioux Falls, SD; **Jennifer Davison,** West Palm Beach, FL; **Lynne M. DiNardo,** Covington, GA; **Kathy Dover,** Lake City, GA; **Cheryl Dultz,** Citrus Heights, CA; **Debbie Friedman,** Fort Lauderdale, FL; **Anne Gaitor,** Lakeland, GA; **Rebecca S. Gillette,** Saint Marys, GA; **Buffy C. Gray,** Peachtree City, GA; **Merry Guest,** Homestead, FL; **Jo Nan Holbrook,** Lakeland, GA; **Beth Holguin,** San Jose, CA; **Coleen Howard-Whals,** St. Petersburg, FL; **Beverly Hurst,** Jacksonville, FL; **Debra Jackson,** St. Petersburg, FL; **Vickie Jordan,** Centerville, GA; **Cheryl Kellogg,** Panama City, FL; **Karen Landers,** Talladega County, AL; **Barb LeFerrier,** Port Orchard, WA; **Sandi Maness,** Modesto, CA; **Ileana Masud,** Miami, FL; **David Miller,** Cooper City, FL; **Muriel Miller,** Simi Valley, CA; **Walsetta W. Miller,** Macon, GA; **Jean Nielson,** Simi Valley, CA; **Sue Patton,** Brea, CA; **Debbie Peale,** Miami, FL; **Loretta Piggee,** Gary, IN; **Jennifer Rader,** Huntington, CA; **April Raiford,** Columbus, GA; **Cheryl Remash,** Manchester, NH; **Francis Rivera,** Orlando, FL; **Marina Rodriguez,** Hialeah, FL; **Marilynn Rose,** MI; **Kathy Scholtz,** Amesbury, MA; **Kimberly Moulton Schorr,** Columbus, GA; **Linda Schrum,** Orlando, FL; **Sharon Searcy,** Mandarin, FL; **Melba Sims,** Orlando, FL; **Judy Smith,** Titusville, FL; **Bea Tamo,** Huntington, CA; **Dottie Thompson,** Jefferson County, AL; **Dana Vassar,** Winston-Salem, NC; **Beverly Wakefield,** Tarpon Springs, FL; **Joy Walls,** Winston-Salem, NC; **Elaine Warwick,** Williamson County, TN; **Audrey N. Watkins,** Atlanta, GA; **Marti Watson,** Sarasota, FL

Supervisors: Judy Artz, Butler County, OH; **James Bennett,** Elkhart, IN; **Kay Buckner-Seal,** Wayne County, MI; **Charlotte Carr,** Seattle, WA; **Sister Marion Christi,** Archdiocese of Philadelphia, PA; **Alvina Crouse,** Denver, CO; **Peggy DeLapp,** Minneapolis, MN; **Carol Erlandson,** Wayne Township Schools, IN; **Brenda Feeney,** North Kansas City School District, MO; **Winnie Huebsch,** Sheboygan, WI; **Brenda Mickey,** Winston-Salem, NC; **Audrey Miller,** Camden, NJ; **JoAnne Piccolo,** Westminster, CO; **Sarah Rentz,** Baton Rouge, LA; **Kathy Sullivan,** Omaha, NE; **Rosie Washington,** Gary, IN; **Theresa Wishart,** Knox County Public Schools, TN

English Language Learners Reviewers: Maria Arevalos, Pomona, CA; **Lucy Blood,** NV; **Manuel Brenes,** Kalamazoo, MI; **Delight Diehn,** AZ; **Susan Dunlap,** Richmond, CA; **Tim Fornier,** Grand Rapids, MI; **Connie Jimenez,** Los Angeles, CA; **Diane Bonilla Lether,** Pasadena, CA; **Anna Lugo,** Chicago, IL; **Marcos Martel,** Hayward, CA; **Carolyn Mason,** Yakima, WA; **Jackie Pinson,** Moorpark, CA; **Jenaro Rivas,** NJ; **Jerilyn Smith,** Salinas, CA; **Noemi Velazquez,** Jersey City, NJ; **JoAnna Veloz,** NJ; **Dr. Santiago Veve,** Las Vegas, NV

CREDITS

Cover
Cover Illustration by Dave Clegg.

Photography
Theme Opener © David Carriere/Index Stock Imagery.

Assignment Photography
© HMCo./Joel Benjamin.

Illustration
T85 Lydia Dabcovich. T143 Francisco Mora.
Theme Class Project art by Tim Johnson.
All other child art by Morgan-Cain & Associates.

ACKNOWLEDGMENTS

Grateful acknowledgment is made for permission to reprint copyrighted material as follows:

Theme 2
I Went Walking, by Sue Williams, illustrated by Julie Vivas. Text copyright © 1989 by Sue Williams. Illustrations copyright © 1989 by Julie Vivas. Reprinted by permission of Harcourt Inc.

ISBN-13: 978-0-618-78411-0
ISBN-10: 0-618-78411-X

1 2 3 4 5 6 7 8 9 10 B 12 11 10 09 08 07 06

Colors All Around

Phonemic Awareness beginning sounds; words in oral sentences

Phonics sounds for *S, s; M, m; R, r*

High-Frequency Words *I, see*

Reading Strategies predict/infer; summarize

Comprehension Skills sequence of events; inferences; making predictions

Vocabulary describing words; exact naming words; singular/plural naming words

Fluency build reading fluency

Concepts of Print capital letters; end punctuation

Writing description; journals; graphic organizer; class story

Listening/Speaking/Viewing supports vocabulary and writing

Colors All Around

CONTENTS

Big Book

Skill Lessons. See Daily Lesson Plans.

Books for Small-Group Reading

Nonfiction

Wordless Book

On My Way Practice Reader
Below Level/On Level
(Week 3)

Leveled Reader
On Level

Little Big Book
On Level/Above Level

Contents **T3**

Theme 2

Bibliography

BOOKS FOR SMALL-GROUP READING, READ ALOUD, AND FLUENCY BUILDING

TARGET SKILL **To build oral language, vocabulary, and fluency,** choose books from this list for additional read aloud opportunities and small-group reading.

Key

	Science
	Social Studies
	Multicultural
	Music
	Math
	Classic
	Art
	Career

Classroom Bookshelf

BOOKS FOR BROWSING

What Color Is Nature?
by Stephen R. Swinburne
Boyds Mills 2002 (32p)
Stunning photographs reveal the many colors found everywhere in nature.

A Rainbow All Around Me
by Sandra L. Pinkney
Scholastic 2002 (32p)
Multiethnic children celebrate the colors of the rainbow and their own diversity.

Little Green
by Keith Baker
Harcourt 2001 (32p)
A boy paints a green hummingbird as it darts and zips around his garden.

Waiting for Wings
by Lois Ehlert
Harcourt 2001 (32p)
After leaving their cocoons, monarch butterflies visit a garden of colorful flowers.

Carlo Likes Colors
by Jessica Spanyol
Candlewick 2003 (32p)
Children learn with Carlo the giraffe as he discovers all the colors in his everyday world.

Lots of Balloons
by Dana Meachen Rau
Compass Point 2002 (32p)
A child buys different color balloons and gives them away to people she meets in the park.

Freight Train
by Donald Crews
Greenwillow 1978 (24p)
A train of colored cars journeys through tunnels, by cities, and over trestles.

Maisy's Rainbow Dream
by Lucy Cousin
Candlewick 2003 (32p)
Maisy's dream journey is full of colorful things like red ladybugs and orange fish.

Tell Me a Season*
by Mary McKenna Siddals
Clarion 1997 (32p)
Simple text describes the colors of the changing seasons.

Kente Colors
by Debbi Chocolate
Walker 1996 (32p) also paper
A celebration of the traditional, colorful kente cloth made by the peoples of Ghana and Togo.

Planting a Rainbow
by Lois Ehlert
Harcourt 1988 (32p) also paper
Planting a garden of flowers, a child learns the colors of the rainbow.

Mouse Paint
by Ellen Stoll Walsh
Harcourt 1989 (32p) also paper
Three white mice experiment with jars of red, yellow, and blue paint. **Available in Spanish as** **Pinta ratones**.

BOOKS FOR TEACHER READ ALOUD

Black All Around!
by Patricia Hubbell
Lee & Low 2003 (32p)
A girl discovers all the wonderful things around her that are black, including cats, beetles, licorice, and Labrador retrievers.

Lunchtime for a Purple Snake
by Harriet Ziefert
Houghton 2003 (32p)
Jessica learns all about colors as she and her artist grandfather paint a picture together.

The Big Red Sled
by Jane E. Gerver
Scholastic 2001 (32p)
Fred the bear should be hibernating, but he takes his red sled out in the snow to play with his animal friends.

Zoe's Hats
by Sharon Lane Holm
Boyds Mills 2003 (32p)
Zoe loves hats and has lots of them in all kinds of colors and patterns.

Harold and the Purple Crayon
by Robert Kraus
Harper 1955 (64p) also paper
A boy draws himself exciting adventures with a purple crayon. **Available in Spanish as** **Harold y el lápiz color morado.**

A Color of His Own
by Leo Lionni
Knopf paper 1997 (32p)
A chameleon goes in search of a color he can call his very own.

*Included in Classroom Bookshelf, Level K

Lilly's Purple Plastic Purse

by Kevin Henkes
Greenwillow 1996 (32p)

The new purple plastic purse Lilly takes to school gets her into trouble.

 Mr. Rabbit and the Lovely Present

by Charlotte Zolotow
Harper 1962 (32p) also paper

A rabbit helps a girl create a colorful birthday gift for her mother. **Available in Spanish as** El señor Conejo y el hermoso regalo.

 Animals Black and White

by Phyllis Limbacher Tildes
Charlesbridge 1996 (32p)

Questions and answers present information on black-and-white animals.

George Paints His House

by Francine Bassède
Orchard 1999 (32p)

George the duck's animal friends give him ideas on what color to paint his house.

A Beasty Story

by Bill Martin Jr.
Harcourt 1999 (32p)

In a rhyming story incorporating color words, four mice who explore a dark house get a surprise.

 Mary Wore Her Red Dress and Henry Wore His Green Sneakers*

by Merle Peek
Clarion 1985 (32p) also paper

On Katy's birthday her animal friends come to the party dressed in clothes of different colors.

 Brown Bear, Brown Bear, What Do You See?

by Bill Martin, Jr.
Holt 1992 (32p)

Animals answer the repeated question "What do you see?" in a playful book about color.

Teeny, Tiny Mouse

by Laura Leuck
Bridgewater 1998 (32p)

A teeny, tiny mouse names objects of various colors he sees around his house.

New Shoes, Red Shoes

by Susan Rollings
Orchard 2000 (32p)

Bouncy verse tells how a girl goes shopping for a new pair of shoes with her mother.

BOOK FOR PHONICS READ ALOUD

 Red Is a Dragon

by Roseanne Thong
Chronicle 2001 (32p)

A girl provides a rhyming description of all the colors she sees around her.

Millie in the Meadow

by Janet Pederson
Candlewick 2003 (32p)

Millie the calf wonders if the artist who paints pictures in the meadow will ever paint one of her.

Rosie's Roses

by Pamela Duncan Edwards
Harper 2003 (32p)

Rosie runs into rotten luck when the roses she buys for Aunt Ruthie's birthday disappear.

Technology

Computer Software Resources

- **Lexia Quick Phonics Assessment CD-ROM**
- **Lexia Phonics Intervention CD-ROM: Primary**
- **Published by Sunburst Technology***
  Tenth Planet™ Vowels: Short and Long
  Curious George® Pre-K ABCs
  First Phonics
- **Published by The Learning Company**
  Dr. Seuss's ABC™

Video Cassettes

- **Harold and the Purple Crayon** *by Robert Krauss. Weston Woods*
- **Dr. Seuss's My Many Colored Days** *by Dr. Seuss. Weston Woods*
- **The Red Balloon** *by Albert Lamorisse. Weston Woods*
- **All the Colors of the Earth** *by Sheila Hamanaka. Weston Woods*
- **A Rainbow of My Own** *by Don Freeman. Weston Woods*
- **Freight Train** *by Donald Crews. SRA Media*

Audio

- **Mary Wore Her Red Dress and Henry Wore His Sneakers** *by Merle Peek. Houghton*
- **Art Dog** *by Thacher Hurd. Live Oak*
- **Caps for Sale** *by Esphyr Slobodkina. Live Oak*
- **Mr. Rabbit and the Lovely Present** *by Charlotte Zolotow. Live Oak*
- **Henry and Mudge Under the Yellow Moon** *by Cynthia Rylant. Live Oak*
- **CD-ROM for *Colors All Around*** *Houghton Mifflin Company*

* *©Sunburst Technology. All Rights Reserved.*
Technology Resources addresses are on page R14.

Education Place

www.eduplace.com *Log on to Education Place for more activities relating to* Colors All Around.

Book Adventure

www.bookadventure.org *This Internet reading incentive program provides thousands of titles for children to read.*

Theme Skills Overview

	Week 1

Teacher Read Aloud
I Need a Lunch Box
Fiction

Big Book
I Went Walking
Concept Book

Pacing
Approximately 3 weeks

Vocabulary Readers

Nonfiction

Leveled Readers

Learning to Read

Phonemic Awareness

Phonics

Concepts of Print

High-Frequency Words

Comprehension

- **Beginning Sounds** T
- **Beginning Sound /s/** T
- **Initial Consonant s** T
- **Concepts of Print** T
- **High-Frequency Word: /** T

Guiding Comprehension

- **Sequence of Events** T
- **Comprehension Strategy: Predict/Infer**
- **Wordless Book**

"My Red Boat"

Science Link *What's My Favorite Color?*
Nonfiction

Books for Small-Group Reading
- Fluency Practice
- Independent Reading

- **Word and Picture Book**
- **Take-Home Phonics Library**
- **Vocabulary Reader**
- **Leveled Reader**
- **Little Big Book**

Word Work

High-Frequency Word Practice

Exploring Words

High-Frequency Word: *I*
- **Color Words**

Writing and Oral Language

Vocabulary

Writing

Listening/Speaking/Viewing

Vocabulary Reader

- **Vocabulary: Using Describing Words**

✏ **Shared Writing:** Writing a Description

Interactive Writing: Writing a Description

Independent Writing: Journals

Listening/Speaking/Viewing

T Skill tested on Emerging Literacy Survey, Integrated Theme Test and/or Weekly or Theme Skills Test

Target Skills

TARGET SKILL

- Phonemic Awareness
- Phonics
- Comprehension
- Vocabulary
- Fluency

Cross-Curricular Activities

Week 1:
Setting Up Centers Activities
Theme Class Project

Week 2:
Setting Up Centers Activities
Theme Class Project

Week 3:
Setting Up Centers Activities
Theme Class Project

Week 2	Week 3: Tested Skill Review

Teacher Read Aloud
Caps of Many Colors
A Traditional Tale

Big Book
In the Big Blue Sea
Nonfiction

Teacher Read Aloud
How the Birds Got Their Colors
A Pourquoi Tale

Big Books
I Went Walking
In the Big Blue Sea

Week 2

- Beginning Sounds T
- Beginning Sound /m/ T
- Initial Consonant *m* T
- Concepts of Print T
- High-Frequency Word: *see* T

Guiding Comprehension

- Inferences: Making Predictions T
- Comprehension Strategy: Summarize
- Wordless Book
"Look at Me!"

Science Link *What Do You Do, Norbert Wu?*
Nonfiction

Week 3: Tested Skill Review

- Beginning Sounds T
- Beginning Sound /r/ T
- Initial Consonant *r* T
- Concepts of Print T
- High-Frequency Words: *I, see* T

Guiding Comprehension

- Sequence of Events T
- Inferences: Making Predictions T
- Comprehension Strategy: Predict/Infer
- Comprehension Strategy: Summarize
- Wordless Book
"The Parade"

Revisit the Links *What's My Favorite Color?* and
What Do You Do, Norbert Wu?

Week 2

- Word and Picture Book
- Take-Home Phonics Library
- Vocabulary Reader
- Leveled Reader
- Little Big Book

Week 3

- On My Way Practice Reader
- Word and Picture Book
- Take-Home Phonics Library
- Vocabulary Reader
- Leveled Reader   Little Big Books

High-Frequency Words: *I, see*

- Color Words

High-Frequency Words: *I, see*

- Color Words

Vocabulary Reader

- Vocabulary: Using Exact Naming Words

✏ **Shared Writing:** Writing a Description

Interactive Writing: Writing a Description

Independent Writing: Journals

Listening/Speaking/Viewing

Vocabulary Reader

- Vocabulary: Using Singular and Plural Words

✏ **Shared Writing:** Writing a Graphic Organizer

Interactive Writing: Writing a Class Story

Independent Writing: Journals

Listening/Speaking/Viewing

Concepts of Print lessons teach important foundational skills for Phonics.

Additional Books for Small-Group Reading

Little Readers for Guided Reading
Use these books to check children's fluency progress.

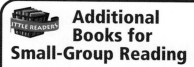

Additional Theme Resources

- Challenge/Extension Activities
- Blackline Masters
- Songs
- Word Lists

Technology

Education Place
www.eduplace.com

Log on to Education Place for more activities relating to *Colors All Around.*

Lesson Planner CD-ROM
Customize your planning for *Colors All Around* with the Lesson Planner CD-ROM.

Curious George® Learns Phonics
Contains interactive phonics activities for beginning readers.

Management Routines

Transition Time

When it is time to move to another activity or to line up, call out different colors of clothing.

- For example, say: "If you have on purple, you may line up," or "Everyone wearing blue may get their snack."
- Children will have to listen carefully to know when they can proceed to the next activity.

Some Transition Suggestions

1. Inform children to wait quietly for instructions.
2. Choose a simple system to organize children, such as clothing color.
3. Call out instructions for children.
4. Children should move quietly as they follow the instructions.
5. Remind children to wait until everyone has been called.
6. Children move to the next activity or space in an orderly fashion.

Instructional Routines

Phonics Center

Show children how to sort **Picture Cards** by beginning sounds. On Day 1, **Alphafriend** *Sammy Seal* will be in the **Phonics Center**, without the letter. Children sort pictures according to whether the beginning sound is /s/ or not /s/. On Day 2, children can make the connection between the letter and the sound it stands for. By the end of the theme, children will sort **Picture Cards** according to the three letters of the theme: *m, r,* and *s.*

Word Wall

Introduce the Word Wall during this theme. Use a classroom wall or bulletin board to post high-frequency words that the children learn. Write each word on a separate card or piece of paper. Designate a "New Words" section on the Word Wall for the words introduced each week. At the end of the week, move the words to a permanent section on the Word Wall. Starting in Theme 4, words with similar spelling patterns can be added in a different color. You might want to organize the words by concepts, spelling patterns, or in some other way. When children need to remember how to write a word they have learned, they can refer to the Word Wall. If you keep a basket filled with blank index cards and markers near your group meeting area, you will have the supplies easily accessible when you write new words to add to the Word Wall.

Theme Class Project

Independent Activities

Have children work on this theme project at any time during the theme while you work with small groups.

Additional Independent Activities

- **Classroom Management Handbook,** pp. 26–49

- **Challenge Handbook,** pp. 2–7

- Setting Up Centers, pp.T22–T23, T68–T69, T116–T117

Color Big Book

Materials 18" x 24" sheets of oaktag • markers • construction paper • color Picture Cards • stapler . . . .

Making Theme Connections

Before beginning the project, display theme resources such as the **Theme Poster,** the **Theme Poem,** and **Big Books.** Begin a discussion about colors children see in the classroom. Then tell children they will write and illustrate a class big book about colors titled *I See.*

What to Do

- Divide the class into small groups, and have each group select a color. Then each group brainstorms a list of things that are the color the children selected. (See Photo #1.)

- To help children focus on their task, you may wish to distribute an item in the color they selected, such as a **Picture Card** or a piece of construction paper.

- Have groups draw pictures of the items they listed on different pieces of oaktag. (See Photo #2.)

- As children work, circulate to help them write the words *I see* and the name of the group's color on each page. They may also want to write other labels. (See Photo #3.)

- When children are finished, staple the book together and read it as a class. If you place the book in your Book Center, children can read it on their own. (See Photo #4.)

- Another kindergarten class may also enjoy visiting your class to read the book. Make sure the children also show the book to their families and friends.

Look for more activities in the **Classroom Management Kit.**

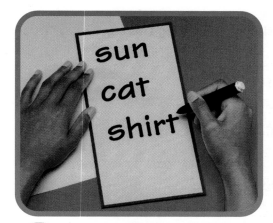

1 Have each group brainstorm a list of things that are the color the children selected.

2 Groups draw pictures of the items they listed on different pieces of oaktag.

3 Write *I see (name of color)* on children's drawings. Some children may wish to add other words.

4 Staple the completed pages into a book.

REACHING ALL LEARNERS

Challenge

Invite children to make suggestions for painting the classroom walls different colors, if they could do so. Suggest they choose a different color for each wall. Then, have children color sheets of paper and paste them to the inside of a box that is roughly shaped like the classroom. Have them invite other classmates to look at the model and share what they think of the new colors for the classroom.

Planning for Assessment

During instruction in Theme 2 . . .

1 SCREENING

To determine children's levels in phonemic awareness, letter recognition, and beginning decoding skills, continue or begin administering the **Emerging Literacy Survey**. Try to test all children by the end of Theme 3.

Section	Areas Assessed
Familiarity with Print	• Concepts of print • Letter naming
Phonemic Awareness	• Rhyme • Beginning sounds • Blending and segmenting onsets and rimes • Blending and segmenting phonemes
Beginning Reading and Writing	• Word recognition • Word writing • Sentence dictation

If children need additional intervention, use the following resource:

• **Teacher's Assessment Handbook,** page 27: support for letter-naming fluency

2 DIAGNOSIS

To determine individual children's specific instructional needs and to plan instruction, administer the following tests:

• **Leveled Reading Passages Assessment Kit**
• **Lexia Quick Phonics Assessment CD-ROM**

3 MONITORING PROGRESS

To ensure that children are making adequate progress throughout the theme, use the following resources:

• Monitoring Student Progress boxes
• Theme 2 Observation Checklist
• Theme 2 **Theme Skills Test**

Kindergarten Benchmarks
Documenting Adequate Yearly Progress

For your planning, listed here are the instructional goals and activities that help develop benchmark behaviors for kindergartners. Use this list to plan instruction and to monitor children's progress. See the checklist of skills found on TE page T185.

Theme Lessons and Activities	Benchmark Behaviors
Listening Comprehension/Oral Language/Vocabulary	
• songs, rhymes, chants, finger plays • story discussions	• listen to a story attentively • participate in story discussions
Phonemic Awareness	
• beginning sounds • syllables in spoken words	• blend sounds into meaningful units
Phonics	
• initial consonants *s, m, r*	• name single letters and their sounds • decode some common CVC words
Concepts of Print	
• capital at the beginning of sentence • end punctuation (period, question mark)	• recognize common print conventions
Reading and Fluency	
• wordless picture books	• tell a story from pictures
Vocabulary: High-Frequency Words	
• high-frequency words *I, see*	• select a letter to represent a sound
Comprehension	
• sequence of events • inferences: making predictions	• think critically about a text • use effective reading strategies
Writing and Language	
• drawing and labeling images • using color words	• label pictures using phonetic spellings • write independently

Launching the Theme

Using the Theme Poster

Read the title of the poster. Tell children that they can see colors everywhere. Point to the fall scene and ask, What colors do you see in this picture? Continue with the pictures for winter, spring, and summer.

Use the poster throughout the theme as a springboard for color activities. Hang the poster in the classroom and have children point to and name different colors during opening routines or during transition times.

- **Week 1:** Children can look at the poster to see if they can find the colors of the shoes, lunchboxes, and pencils from *I Need a Lunch Box.*

- **Week 2:** After reading *In the Big Blue Sea,* have children tell which color of fish they liked the best, and why.

- **Week 3:** After rereading *I Went Walking,* have small groups talk about nature walks they have taken and the colorful animals that they saw along the way.

Theme Poem: "I Love Colors"

Read the poem aloud.

- Ask, What do you notice about some of the words in the poem? Point out that the color words are printed in the color of the word names.

- Read the poem again, then have children echo-read. After several readings, name a color word and have a child point to the correct word.

Read aloud other poems. Poems help develop children's oral comprehension and listening skills. You may want to choose other poems to read aloud from *Higglety Pigglety: A Book of Rhymes*.

Higglety Pigglety: A Book of Rhymes, page 10

Monitoring Student Progress

Monitoring Progress

Throughout the theme, monitor your children's progress by using the following program features in the **Teacher's Edition**:

- Guiding Comprehension questions
- Literature response groups
- Skill lesson applications
- Monitoring Student Progress boxes
- Theme Wrap-Up, pages T184–T185

Classroom Management

At any time during the theme, you can assign the Theme Class Project on **Teacher Edition** pages T10–T11 while you provide differentiated instruction to small groups.

Additional independent activity centers related to specific selections can be found in the **Teacher's Edition**.

- Setting Up Centers, Week 1, pages T22–T23
- Setting Up Centers, Week 2, pages T78–T79
- Setting Up Centers, Week 3, pages T136–T137

Home Connection

Send home the theme newsletter for *Colors All Around* to introduce the theme and suggest home activities (See **Teacher's Resource Blackline Masters** 27–28.)

For other suggestions relating to *Colors All Around*, see **Home/Community Connections.**

Lesson Overview

Literature

HOUGHTON MIFFLIN
Reading

I Went Walking

WRITTEN BY
Sue Williams

ILLUSTRATED BY
Julie Vivas

Includes:
Science Link

Selection Summary

While taking a walk, a young boy has farm animals of different colors join him.

1 Teacher Read Aloud

• *I Need a Lunch Box*

2 Big Book

• *I Went Walking*
  Genre: Concept Book

3 Wordless Book

Phonics Library

• "My Red Boat"

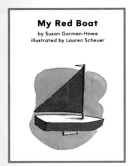

4 Science Link

This Link appears after the main Big Book selection.

Leveled Books

Vocabulary Reader

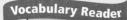

- Below Level, ELL
- Lesson

Leveled Reader

- On Level, Above Level
- Lesson
- Take-Home Version

Plus!
Online Leveled Books

Instructional Support

Planning and Practice

Tennessee Teacher's Edition

Teacher's Resources

Alphafriends

Practice book

Ready-Made Centers

Phonics Center

Building Vocabulary

Reading in Science and Social Studies
- 30 books and activities
- support for Tennessee content standards

Hands-On Literacy Centers for Week 1
- activities
- manipulatives
- routines

Differentiated Instruction

Intervention/Extra Support

English Language Learners

Technology

 Audio Selection
I Went Walking

 *Curious George Learns Phonics*

www.eduplace.com
- over 1,000 Online Leveled Books

Challenge

Daily Lesson Plans

T Skill tested on Weekly or Theme Skills Test and/or Integrated Theme Test

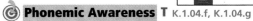 Tennessee Curriculum Standards indicated in blue.

DAILY LESSON PLANS

WEEK 1

60–90 minutes

Learning to Read

Phonemic Awareness

Phonics

High-Frequency Words

Comprehension

Concepts of Print

Leveled Reader

DAY 1

K.1.01.b, K.1.02.b, K.1.01.g
Daily Routines, *T24–T25*
Calendar, Message

Phonemic Awareness T K.1.04.f, K.1.04.g

Teacher Read Aloud, *T26–T27* K.1.02.a, K.1.02.b

Comprehension Strategy, *T26* K.1.08.c
Predict/Infer

Comprehension Skill, *T26* K.1.09.b.1
Sequence of Events **T**

Phonemic Awareness, *T28–T29* K.1.04.f
Beginning Sound /s/ **T**

Cross-Curricular Activity, T23 SC.K.5.2

Leveled Reader
K.1.06, K.1.07, K.1.09.a

DAY 2

K.1.01.b, K.1.02.b
Daily Routines, *T32–T33*
Calendar, Message

Phonemic Awareness T K.1.04.f, K.1.04.g

Reading the Big Book, *T34–T35* K.1.08.b, K.1.08.

Comprehension Strategy, *T34*
Predict/Infer K.1.08.c, K.1.08.d

Comprehension Skill, *T34* K.1.09.b.1
Sequence of Events **T**

Phonics, *T36–T37* K.1.04.f, K.2.02.a
Initial Consonant *s* **T**

High-Frequency Word, *T38–T39*
New Word: *I* **T** K.1.06.a, K.1.07.a

Leveled Reader
K.1.06, K.1.07, K.1.09.a

30–45 minutes

Word Work

Exploring Words

Exploring Words, *T40* K.1.07.a
Color Words

Exploring Words, *T40* K.1.07.a
Color Words

30–45 minutes

Writing and Oral Language

Vocabulary

Writing

Listening/Speaking/ Viewing

Oral Language: Vocabulary, *T31* K.1.01.a
Using Describing Words

Vocabulary Reader K.1.07.a

Vocabulary Reader K.1.07.a

Vocabulary Expansion, *T31* K.1.01.a
Using Describing Words

Listening/Speaking/Viewing, *T41* K.1.01.f, K.1.01.e, K.1.01.c

---

 Half-Day Kindergarten

Focus on lessons for tested skills marked with **T**. Then choose other activities as time allows.

Tennessee English/Language Arts Curriculum Standards
and
Houghton Mifflin Reading

Grade K

For use with each Daily Lesson Plan

Grade K Learning Expectations

Reading

K.1.01 Develop oral language.
K.1.02 Develop listening skills.
K.1.03 Demonstrate knowledge of concepts of print.
K.1.04 Develop and maintain phonemic awareness.
K.1.05 Develop and use decoding strategies to read unfamiliar words.
K.1.06 Read to develop fluency, expression, accuracy, and confidence.
K.1.07 Develop and extend reading vocabulary.
K.1.08 Develop and use pre-reading strategies.
K.1.09 Use active comprehension strategies to derive meaning while reading and check for understanding after reading.
K.1.10 Introduce informational skills to facilitate learning.
K.1.11 Develop skills to facilitate reading to learn in a variety of content areas.
K.1.12 Read independently for a variety of purposes.
K.1.13 Experience various literary genres.
K.1.14 Develop and maintain a motivation to read.

Writing

K.2.01 Use a variety of pre-writing strategies.
K.2.02 Write for a variety of purposes.
K.2.03 Show evidence of drafting and revision with written work.
K.2.04 Include editing before the completion of finished work.
K.2.05 Evaluate own and others' writing.
K.2.06 Experience numerous publishing opportunities.
K.2.07 Write narrative accounts.
K.2.08 Write frequently across content areas.
K.2.09 Write expressively using original ideas, reflections, and observations.
K.2.10 Write in response to literature.
K.2.11 Write in a variety of modes and genres.

Elements of Language

K.3.01 Demonstrate knowledge of standard English usage.
K.3.02 Demonstrate knowledge of standard English mechanics.
K.3.03 Demonstrate knowledge of standard English spelling.
K.3.04 Demonstrate knowledge of correct sentence structure.

Curriculum Standards Achieved in Theme 2

Week 1: I Need a Lunch Box / I Went Walking

Daily Lesson Plans, T18–T19

I   **K.1.01.a** Expand oral language
I   **K.1.01.b** Speak clearly/properly/politely
I   **K.1.01.c** Begin to use rules for conversation
I   **K.1.01.e** Participate in group discussion
I   **K.1.01.f** Creative responses to text
I   **K.1.01.g** Ask/respond to teacher questions
I   **K.1.01.h** Begin to retell familiar stories
I   **K.1.02.a** Listen for specific information
I   **K.1.02.b** Use appropriate listening skills
I   **K.1.04.f** Words: same beginning/ending sound
I   **K.1.04.g** Know words made up of syllables
I   **K.1.06** Read to develop fluency
I   **K.1.06.a** Letter-sound/high-frequency words
I   **K.1.07** Develop and extend reading vocabulary

I   **K.1.07.a** Build vocabulary: listen/participate
I   **K.1.07.f** Use a picture dictionary
I   **K.1.08.b** Relate background knowledge
I   **K.1.08.c** Make predictions about text
I   **K.1.08.d** Use illustrations to preview text
I   **K.1.08.e** Create graphic organizers
I   **K.1.08.f** Connect text to life experience
I   **K.1.09.a** Derive meaning while reading
I   **K.1.09.b.1** Recall sequence of events
I   **K.1.13.a** Explore picture books
I   **K.2.02.a** Write to acquire/exhibit knowledge
I   **K.2.08.d** Shared writing: arts/personal life
I   **K.3.02.d** Recognize ending punctuation marks
I   **K.3.02.e** Capitalize at beginning of sentence
    SC.K.5.2 Features help living things survive

Blueprint for Learning Key:
A = Assessed, **I** = Introduced, **M** = Maintained or Mastered, **D** = Developing
SC = Science, **SS** = Social Studies

continues

186510

Curriculum Standards Achieved in Theme 2

Week 2: Caps of Many Colors / In the Big Blue Sea

Daily Lesson Plans, T74–T75

I	**K.1.01.a**	Expand oral language
I	**K.1.01.c**	Begin to use rules for conversation
I	**K.1.01.e**	Participate in group discussion
I	**K.1.01.f**	Creative responses to text
I	**K.1.01.g**	Ask/respond to teacher questions
I	**K.1.01.h**	Begin to retell familiar stories
I	**K.1.04.f**	Words: same beginning/ending sound
I	**K.1.04.g**	Know words made up of syllables
I	**K.1.06**	Read to develop fluency
I	**K.1.06.a**	Letter-sound/high-frequency words
I	**K.1.07**	Develop and extend reading vocabulary
I	**K.1.07.a**	Build vocabulary: listen/participate
I	**K.1.08.c**	Make predictions about text
I	**K.1.08.d**	Use illustrations to preview text
I	**K.1.09.a**	Derive meaning while reading
I	**K.1.09.b.2**	Retell story in own words
I	**K.1.12.a**	Read to gain information
I	**K.1.13.a**	Explore picture books
I	**K.1.14.c**	Identify favorite stories
I	**K.2.01.a**	Brainstorm ideas with teacher/peers
I	**K.2.02.a**	Write to acquire/exhibit knowledge
I	**K.2.02.b**	Write to entertain
I	**K.2.03.d**	Add descriptive words/details
I	**K.2.07.b**	Express thoughts: writing/illustrating
I	**K.2.10.c**	Respond with drawing/picture/graphic
I	**K.2.11.a**	Illustrate and/or write in journals
I	**K.3.01.b**	Use correct verb/verb tense
I	**K.3.02**	Demonstrate mechanics of English
I	**K.3.02.d**	Recognize ending punctuation marks
I	**K.3.02.e**	Capitalize at beginning of sentence
I	**K.3.04**	Knowledge of sentence structure
	SC.K.5.2	Features help living things survive

Week 3: How the Birds Got Their Colors / I Went Walking / In the Big Blue Sea

Daily Lesson Plans, T132–T133

I	**K.1.01.a**	Expand oral language
I	**K.1.01.e**	Participate in group discussion
I	**K.1.01.g**	Ask/respond to teacher questions
I	**K.1.02.a**	Listen for specific information
I	**K.1.02.b**	Use appropriate listening skills
I	**K.1.03.b**	Understand print has meaning
I	**K.1.03.e**	Identify front cover/back cover of a book
I	**K.1.04.e**	Recognize and produce rhyming words
I	**K.1.04.f**	Words: same beginning/ending sound
I	**K.1.04.g**	Know words made up of syllables
I	**K.1.06**	Read to develop fluency
I	**K.1.06.a**	Letter-sound/high-frequency words
I	**K.1.07**	Develop and extend reading vocabulary
I	**K.1.07.a**	Build vocabulary: listen/participate
I	**K.1.08.a**	Recognize purpose for listening
I	**K.1.08.c**	Make predictions about text
I	**K.1.08.d**	Use illustrations to preview text
I	**K.1.09.a**	Derive meaning while reading
I	**K.1.09.b.1**	Recall sequence of events
I	**K.1.09.b.2**	Retell story in own words
I	**K.1.09.b.4**	Use pictures to discuss main idea
I	**K.1.12.a**	Read to gain information
I	**K.1.12.b**	Read for enjoyment
I	**K.1.13.a**	Explore picture books
I	**K.2.01.c**	Construct graphic organizers
I	**K.2.02.a**	Write to acquire/exhibit knowledge
I	**K.2.02.b**	Write to entertain
I	**K.2.10.c**	Respond with drawing/picture/graphic
I	**K.2.11.a**	Illustrate and/or write in journals
I	**K.3.02**	Demonstrate mechanics of English
I	**K.3.02.d**	Recognize ending punctuation marks
I	**K.3.02.e**	Capitalize at beginning of sentence
	SC.K.5.2	Features help living things survive

Lesson Planner CD-ROM
Develop and customize your own lesson plans with the Tennessee Lesson Planner CD-ROM

Blueprint for Learning Key:
A = Assessed, **I** = Introduced, **M** = Maintained or Mastered, **D** = Developing
SC = Science, **SS** = Social Studies

186510

Target Skills of the Week

Phonemic Awareness	Beginning Sounds; Words in Oral Sentences
Phonics	Initial Consonant *Ss*
Comprehension	Sequence of Events; Predict/Infer
Vocabulary	High-Frequency Words; Color Words; Describing Words
Fluency	Phonics Library

DAY 3

K.1.01.g, K.1.02.b, K.2.02.a, K.1.06.a

My Red Boat
by Susan Gorman-Howe
illustrated by Lauren Scheuer

Daily Routines, *T42–T43*
Calendar, Message,
High–Frequency Words

Phonemic Awareness **T** K.1.04.f, K.1.04.g

Reading the Big Book, *T44–T49*
K.1.09.b.1, K.3.02.e, K.3.02.d
Comprehension Strategy, *T45, T46*
Predict/Infer K.1.08.c

Comprehension Skill, *T45, T47, T48*
Sequence of Events **T** K.1.09.b.1

Concepts of Print, *T46*
Capitalize First Word in Sentence;
End Punctuation **T** K.3.02.d, K.3.02.e

Phonics, *T50* K.1.04.f
Initial Consonant *s* **T**

Storytelling Practice, *T51–T53*
"My Red Boat" K.1.04.f, K.1.08.c, K.1.08.d,
K.1.01.h, K.1.13.a

Vocabulary Reader K.1.07.a

Leveled Reader
K.1.06, K.1.07, K.1.09.a

Exploring Words, *T54*
Color Words K.1.08.e, K.1.07.a, K.1.01.f

Shared Writing, *T55* K.2.08.d, K.1.01.c
Writing a Description

DAY 4

K.1.01.a, K.1.04.f, K.1.06.a

We read a magazine.

Daily Routines, *T56–T57*
Calendar, Message,
High–Frequency Words

Phonemic Awareness **T** K.1.04.f, K.1.04.g

Reading the Science Link, *T58–T59*

Comprehension Strategy, *T58* K.1.08.c
Predict/Infer

Comprehension Skill, *T58–T59* K.1.09.b.1
Sequence of Events **T**

Concepts of Print, *T59* K.3.02.d, K.3.02.e
Capitalize First Word in Sentence;
End Punctuation **T**

Phonics, *T60–T61* K.1.04.f
Initial Consonant *s* **T**

Vocabulary Reader K.1.07.a

Leveled Reader
K.1.06, K.1.07, K.1.09.a

Exploring Words, *T62*
Color Words K.1.08.e, K.1.07.e, K.2.01.a

Interactive Writing, *T63* K.2.02.c, K.2.07.a
Writing a Description

DAY 5

K.1.01.e, K.3.02.d,
K.3.02.e, K.1.06.a

I Went Walking
I NEED A LUNCH BOX
My Red Boat

Daily Routines,
T64–T65
Calendar, Message,
High–Frequency Words

Phonemic Awareness **T** K.1.04.f, K.1.04.g

Revisiting the Literature, *T66*
K.1.09.b.2, K.1.09.b.1, K.1.14.c

Comprehension Skill, *T66* K.1.09.b.1
Sequence of Events **T**

Storytelling, *T67* K.1.09.b.2

Phonics Review, *T68* K.1.04.f
Initial Consonant *s* **T**

High-Frequency Word Review, *T69*
Word: *I* **T** K.1.06.a, K.3.04.b

Word and Picture Book, *T69*
K.1.13.a, K.1.12.a, K.1.01.e

Vocabulary Reader K.1.07.a

Leveled Reader
K.1.06, K.1.07, K.1.09.a

Exploring Words, *T70*
Color Words K.1.01.f, K.1.01.e, K.1.07.a

Independent Writing, *T71* K.2.11.a
Journals

Concepts of Print lessons teach important foundational skills for Phonics.

Managing Flexible Groups

Leveled Instruction and Leveled Practice

WHOLE CLASS

DAY 1

- Daily Routines (TE pp. T24–T25)
- Teacher Read Aloud: *I Need a Lunch Box* (TE pp. T26–T27)
- Phonemic Awareness (TE pp. T28–T29)

DAY 2

- Daily Routines (TE pp. T32–T33)
- Big Book: *I Went Walking* (TE pp. T34–T35)
- Phonics lesson (TE pp. T36–T37)
- High-Frequency Word lesson (TE pp. T38–T39)

SMALL GROUPS

Organize small groups according to children's needs.

DAY 1

TEACHER-LED GROUPS

- Begin Practice Book pp. 71–72, 73–74. (TE pp. T27, T29)
- Introduce Phonics Center. (TE p. T29)
- Leveled Reader

DAY 2

TEACHER-LED GROUPS

- Begin Practice Book pp. 75, 76. (TE pp. T37, T39)
- Write letters *S, s*; begin handwriting Blackline Masters 175 or 201. (TE p. T37)
- Introduce Phonics Center. (TE p. T37)
- Leveled Reader
- Vocabulary Reader

DAY 1

INDEPENDENT GROUPS

- Complete Practice Book pp. 71–72, 73–74. (TE pp. T27, T29)
- Use Phonics Center. (TE p. T29)

DAY 2

INDEPENDENT GROUPS

- Complete Practice Book pp. 75, 76. (TE pp. T37, T39)
- Complete Blackline Masters 175 or 201.
- Use Phonics Center. (TE p. T37)

English Language Learners
Support is provided in the Reaching All Learners notes throughout the week.

Independent Activities

- Complete Practice Book pages 71–79.
- Complete penmanship practice (Teacher's Resource Blackline Master 175 or 201).
- Retell familiar Phonics Library or Word and Picture Book stories.
- Share trade books from Leveled Bibliography. (See pp. T4–T5)

DAY 3

- Daily Routines (TE pp. T42–T43)
- Big Book: *I Went Walking* (TE pp. T44–T49)
- Phonics lesson (TE p. T50)

TEACHER-LED GROUPS

- Begin Practice Book p. 77. (TE p. T49)
- Tell Phonics Library: "My Red Boat." (TE pp. T51–T53)
- Leveled Reader
- Vocabulary Reader

INDEPENDENT GROUPS

- Complete Practice Book pp. 77. (TE p. T49)
- **Fluency Practice** Retell Phonics Library: "My Red Boat." (TE pp. T51–T53)

DAY 4

- Daily Routines (TE pp. T56–T57)
- Science Link: *What's My Favorite Color?* (TE pp. T58–T59)
- Phonics lesson (TE pp. T60–T61)

TEACHER-LED GROUPS

- Begin Practice Book p. 78. (TE p. T61)
- Introduce Phonics Center. (TE p. T61)
- Leveled Reader
- Vocabulary Reader

INDEPENDENT GROUPS

- Complete Practice Book p. 78. (TE p. T61)
- **Fluency Practice** Color and reread Phonics Library: "My Red Boat." (TE pp. T51–T53)
- Use Phonics Center. (TE p. T61)

DAY 5

- Daily Routines (TE pp. T64–T65)
- Retelling (TE pp. T66–T67)
- Phonics and High-Frequency Word Review (TE pp. T68–T69)

TEACHER-LED GROUPS

- Begin Practice Book p. 79. (TE p. T69)
- Read Word and Picture Book: *I* 🏃.
- **Fluency Practice** Retell the Take-Home version of "My Red Boat."
- Leveled Reader
- Vocabulary Reader

INDEPENDENT GROUPS

- Complete Practice Book p. 79. (TE p. T69)
- **Fluency Practice** Reread Word and Picture Book: *I* 🏃. Retell a favorite Phonics Library or Leveled Reader story.

- Retell or reread Little Big Books.
- Listen to Big Book Audio CDs.
- Use the Phonics Center and other Centers. (See pp. T22–T23)

Turn the page for more independent activities.

Managing Flexible Groups T21

Ready-Made for Tennessee

Building Vocabulary

ELA.K.1.01.a, ELA.K.1.01.e,
ELA.K.1.01.f, ELA.K.1.01.g,
ELA.K.1.07.a, ELA.K.1.07.b

Center Activity 4

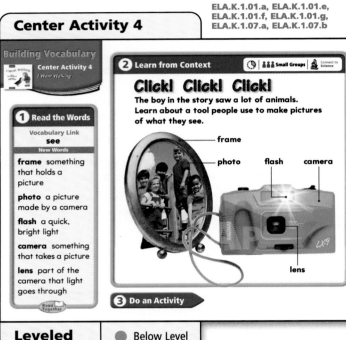

Building Vocabulary
Center Activity 4
I Went Walking

2 Learn from Context ⏱ 👥 Small Groups | 🔬 Connect to Science

Click! Click! Click!
The boy in the story saw a lot of animals.
Learn about a tool people use to make pictures
of what they see.

frame
photo   flash   camera
lens

1 Read the Words

Vocabulary Link
see
New Words

frame something that holds a picture

photo a picture made by a camera

flash a quick, bright light

camera something that takes a picture

lens part of the camera that light goes through

3 Do an Activity ▶

Leveled Activities
on back of card

● Below Level
▲ On Level
■ Above Level

Hands-On Literacy Centers
I Went Walking

Challenge and Routine Cards

Sorting Pictures

Materials

① Look.   ② Say.   ③ Sort.

2. Animals Everywhere
What animals could you see at the zoo or in the forest?

TIP
• Use books and charts to help you write the words.

• ___ a picture of an animal you could see.
• ___ the name and color of the animal.

3. My Perfect Lunch Box
What would your perfect lunch box look like?

TIP
• Use your imagination.

• ___ a picture of your perfect lunch box.
• ___ about your lunch box.

Manipulatives

I

Reading in Science

Independent Book
Mouse's Meadow
Students apply comprehension skills to fiction text.

Mouse's Meadow
by Deborah Akers

SC.K.5.2, ELA.K.1.1.09.b.2

Center Activity 4

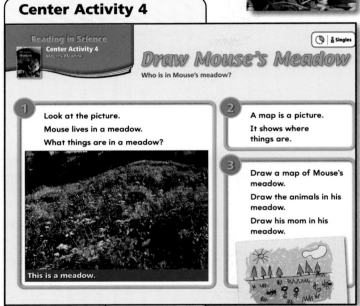

Reading in Science
Center Activity 4
Mouse's Meadow

⏱ 👤 Singles

Draw Mouse's Meadow
Who is in Mouse's meadow?

① Look at the picture.
Mouse lives in a meadow.
What things are in a meadow?

This is a meadow.

② A map is a picture.
It shows where things are.

③ Draw a map of Mouse's meadow.
Draw the animals in his meadow.
Draw his mom in his meadow.

Leveled Activities
on back of card

● Below Level
▲ On Level
■ Above Level

More Nonfiction Reading

School Days Long Ago and Today

Fun and Games

Save Our Tree
by Leslie Sullivan

Am Water
by K.O. Amanda

30 topics aligned with Tennessee Science and Social Studies standards!

MADE FOR TENNESSEE

Setting Up Centers

Writing Center

Materials
drawing paper, Blackline Master 35

Children create their own books about color. They draw illustrations and label them with color words. Children also write color words and draw a picture to complete Blackline Master 35. See pages T31 and T63 for this week's Writing Center activities.

SC.K.12.1

Science Center

Materials
picture books of farm animals, drawing paper, crayons

Children work in groups as they browse through the books and make a picture list of the animals they see. See page T35 for this week's Science Center activity

SC.K.5.2

Art Center

Materials
Blackline Master 34, cups of red, blue, and yellow paint, paint brushes

Children draw pictures of animals in their neighborhood. Later in the week, small groups record what happens when they mix different colors of paint. See pages T41 and T49 for this week's Art Center activities.

SC.K.12.1

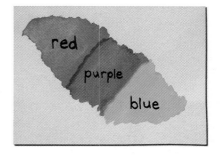

DAY 1
week 1

Day at a Glance
T24–T31

Learning to Read

Teacher Read Aloud, *T26*
Phonemic Awareness: /s/, *T28*

Word Work

Exploring Words, *T30*

Writing & Oral Language

Oral Language, *T31*

Daily Routines

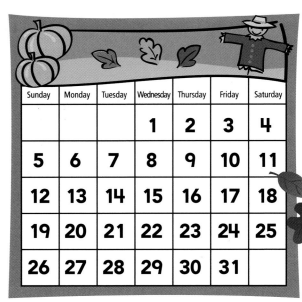

Sunday	Monday	Tuesday	Wednesday	Thursday	Friday	Saturday
			1	2	3	4
5	6	7	8	9	10	11
12	13	14	15	16	17	18
19	20	21	22	23	24	25
26	27	28	29	30	31	

Calendar

Reading the Calendar
Conduct your calendar routine, having children repeat the names of the days of the week after you. Call on individuals to name different colors on the calendar.

Daily Message

Modeled Writing
Celebrate starting a new reading theme by including the theme title in your daily message. Discuss with children the colors they see around them. Remind them to speak in complete sentences.

Today we start a new theme called <u>Colors All Around</u>. Brian has a new green sweater today.

Daily Phonemic Awareness

Beginning Sounds

- Listen: *sssix, sssoap*. Say the words with me: *six, soap*. Do you hear the same sound at the beginning of each word? . . . So do I. *Six* and *soap* begin with the same sound.

- Have children play Same Sound Sort. If the words begin with the same sound, raise your hands. If the words do not begin with the same sound, cover your ears. Continue with the words shown.

bike/bell	cat/dog
milk/mouse	rock/room
sock/sun	ten/top
nest/nose	sink/mop

Words in Oral Sentences

- Read aloud "Blowing Bubbles," page 8 of *Higglety Pigglety: A Book of Rhymes*.

- Listen to my sentence from the poem: "Dip your pipe and gently blow." Let's clap each time we hear a word. How many claps?

- This time, draw a line for each word. Count the marks.

Getting Ready to Learn

To help children plan their day, tell them that they will–

- listen to a story called *I Need a Lunch Box*.

- meet an Alphafriend.

- learn more about colors and color words in the Book Center.

OBJECTIVES

- Develop oral language (listening, responding).
- Preview comprehension skill.

Read Aloud
HOUGHTON MIFFLIN
Reading

Jeannette Caines
I NEED A LUNCH BOX

pictures by
Pat Cummings

I Need a Lunch Box

Selection Summary A young boy is envious when his older sister gets a new lunch box for school. His fascination with lunch boxes grows until, on the first day of school, his father surprises him with a lunch box.

Key Concepts

Colors

Days of the week

Needs and wants

English Language Learners

Before you read, review or introduce colors and the days of the week.

Teacher Read Aloud

Building Background

If you have one, show a lunch box or an insulated lunch bag. Talk about what it is used for, how it is packed, and what children like or don't like about it.

TARGET SKILL COMPREHENSION STRATEGY

Predict/Infer

Display *I Need a Lunch Box*. Read aloud the names of the author and illustrator. Allow children to comment on the title and the cover illustration.

Teacher Modeling Model the strategy for predicting what a book will be about.

Think Aloud How can I tell what *I Need a Lunch Box* is about?

- I can look at the cover. Maybe this is the boy who needs a lunch box.
- I wonder why the boy needs a lunch box. Maybe he's going to school. What do you think? Let's read to find out.

TARGET SKILL COMPREHENSION SKILL

Sequence of Events

Teacher Modeling Tell children that things in a story happen in a certain order.

Think Aloud It's important to think about the order as you read. I'll pay attention to what happens first, next, and last in the story. You can help me do that. Listen as I read.

Listening to the Story

As you read, help children imagine that the boy is actually telling the story.

Responding

Oral Language: Summarizing the Story Help children summarize parts of the story.

- Did the boy really need a lunch box? Why do you think he wanted one? Did you ever want something you didn't really need?

- What did Doris get to take to school? Why didn't the boy get these things? How did he feel about that?

- Why do you think the boy dreamed of lunch boxes? What colors did he dream about?

- How does the story end? Were we right when we predicted the boy needed a lunch box for school?

Practice Book Children will complete **Practice Book** pages 71–72 during small group time.

Practice Book page 71

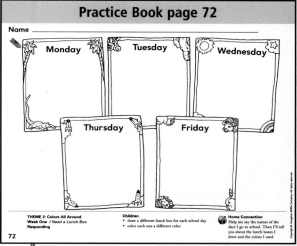

Practice Book page 72

Book Center

Have a rainbow of color books available in the Book Center. Include favorites like *Brown Bear, Brown Bear, What Do You See?* by Bill Martin, Jr. and *Freight Train* by Donald Crews. Other good choices for exploring colors include *Planting a Rainbow* by Lois Ehlert, *Kente Colors* by Debbi Chocolate, *Mouse Paint* by Ellen Stoll Walsh, and *Animals Black and White* by Phyllis Limbacher Tildes.

OBJECTIVES

- Identify pictures whose names begin with /s/.

Materials

- **Alphafriend Cards** *Sammy Seal*
- **Alphafriend CD** Theme 2
- **Alphafolder** *Sammy Seal*
- **Picture Cards** boat, man, rock, sandbox, sandwich, six, sun, ten
- **Phonics Center** Theme 2, Week 1, Day 1

Alphafolder *Sammy Seal*

Home Connection

Hand out the take-home version of Sammy Seal's Song. Ask children to share the song with their families. (See **Alphafriends Blackline Masters**.)

 English Language Learners

Children may confuse the /s/ and /z/ sounds. Display **Picture Cards** for *s* and ask children to repeat the names aloud. Make sure children know the *s* words in Sammy Seal's song: *seal, sea, sail, seagull, salutes, season, sunny, summer.*

PHONEMIC AWARENESS
Beginning Sound

❶ Teach

Introduce Alphafriend: Sammy Seal
Use the Alphafriend routine to introduce Sammy Seal.

▶ **Alphafriend Riddle**
Read these clues:

- Our new Alphafriend's sound is /s/. Say it with me: /s/.
- This animal *ssswims* and dives in the *sssea* all day long.
- He has flippers instead of hands and feet, but he barks like a dog.
- You might *sssee* him balance a ball at the aquarium or the zoo.

When most hands are up, call on children until they name *seal*.

▶ **Pocket Chart** Display Sammy Seal in a pocket chart. Explain that Sammy's sound is /s/. Say his name, emphasizing the /s/ sound slightly, and have children echo this.

▶ **Alphafriend CD** Play Sammy Seal's song. Listen for /s/ words.

▶ **Alphafolder** Have children look at the scene and name all the /s/ words.

▶ **Summarize**

- What is our Alphafriend's name? What is his sound?
- What words in our Alphafriend's song start with /s/?
- Each time you look at Sammy Seal this week, remember the /s/ sound.

Sammy Seal's Song
(tune: Yankee Doodle)

Sammy Seal will sail the sea
    when summer is the season.

Sammy Seal will sail the sea
    and never need a reason.

Sammy Seal will sail the sea
    in very sunny weather.

Sammy Seal salutes a seagull
    as they sail together!

❷ Guided Practice

Listen for /s/ and compare sounds. Tell children you'll hold up and name some **Picture Cards** and they should signal "thumbs up" for each one that begins like Sammy's name.

Have children put the cards below Sammy's picture. If the picture doesn't begin like Sammy, children should signal "thumbs down," and leave the card in the bottom row.

Pictures: *sandwich, man, ten, six, rock, sun, boat, sandbox*

Tell children that they will sort more pictures in the **Phonics Center** today.

❸ Apply

Have children complete **Practice Book** pages 73–74 at small group time.

Practice Book page 73

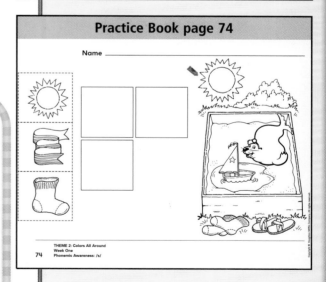

Practice Book page 74

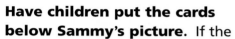

 **Phonics** Center

Materials Phonics Center materials for Theme 2, Week 1, Day 1 ....

Display Day 1 Direction Chart. Children put *Sammy Seal* (no letter) in separate sections of Workmat 2. Then they sort remaining pictures by initial sound: /s/ and not /s/.

- Explore color words.
- Create a class color graph.

- *From Apples to Zebras: A Book of ABC's,* page 29
- Teacher-made rectangles of colored paper for class graph

INSTRUCTION

EXPLORING WORDS
Color Words

Name color words together.

- Display *From Apples to Zebras: A Book of ABC's,* page 29. What do you see? That's right, colors. Name them with me. Point to each color and name it with children. Check to see how aware of color words children seem to be.

- Now tell children to watch as you point to the color words. Explain that each color has a name that you can read.

- Have each child name a favorite color and choose a color square to represent it.

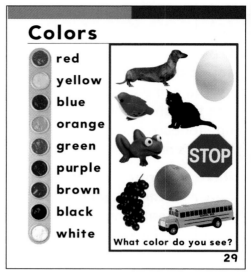

From Apples to Zebras: A Book of ABC's, page 29

Create a graph of favorite colors.
Ask each child to write his or her name on the square and, if they choose, to copy the color word. Ask all children with a red square of paper to place their squares on the graph. Continue in the same manner until all children have contributed to the graph.

Discuss the graph.
How many children like blue? How many children like green? Which color is liked by the most children?

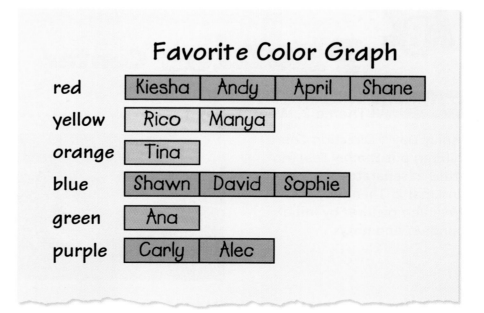

Favorite Color Graph

red	Kiesha	Andy	April	Shane
yellow	Rico	Manya		
orange	Tina			
blue	Shawn	David	Sophie	
green	Ana			
purple	Carly	Alec		

ORAL LANGUAGE: VOCABULARY
Using Describing Words

❶ Teach

Discuss describing words.

- Read aloud "I Love Colors," page 10 of *Higglety Pigglety: A Book of Rhymes.*

- Explain that color words tell about how something looks.

- Read the poem again, asking children to listen for the color words.

❷ Practice/Apply

Have children practice using describing words. Have children take turns placing the **Picture Cards** and color **Word Cards** in a pocket chart as you point to and read each color word in the poem.

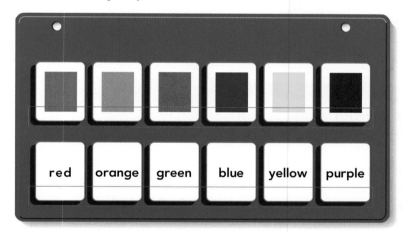

| red | orange | green | blue | yellow | purple |

✏️ Writing Center

Hang the pocket chart in the Writing Center. Have children make color books by drawing pictures to illustrate different colors. They can refer to the **Word Cards** to help them label each page with a color word. Have children write each color word in the appropriate color.

Red

OBJECTIVES
- Use color words to describe.
- Illustrate and label color books.

Materials
- *Higglety Pigglety: A Book of Rhymes,* page 10
- **Word Cards** color words
- **Picture Cards** *blue, green, orange, purple, red, yellow, black, white*

DAY 2
week 1

Day at a Glance
T32–T41

Learning to Read

Big Book, *T34*
Phonics: Initial Consonant *s, T36*
High Frequency Word: *I, T38*

Word Work

Exploring Words, *T40*

Writing & Oral Language

Vocabulary Expansion, *T41*

Daily Routines

Calendar

Reading the Calendar Choose a color for each day of the week. Have children wear or bring in something of that color to celebrate the day.

Sunday	Monday	Tuesday	Wednesday	Thursday	Friday	Saturday
			1	2	3	4
5	6	7	8	9	10	11
12	13	14	15	16	17	18
19	20	21	22	23	24	25
26	27	28	29	30	31	

Daily Message

Modeled Writing
As you write the daily message, describe what you are doing. **The first word I want to write is** *today.* *Today* **is also the first word in my sentence so I will begin it with a capital letter.**

Today we have art at 10:00. What colors will we mix?

 Daily Phonemic Awareness

Beginning Sounds

- Display **Picture Cards** *bat*, *bike*, *jar*, *jeep*, *rake*, *red*, *pan*, and *peach*. Have children name the pictures. Then hold up and name **Picture Card** *bat*. Say the word with me.

- Look for a picture that starts with the same sound as *bat*. Is it *jeep*? Is it *rake*? Is it *bike*? Yes, it's *bike*. Say the two words together.

- Continue with other **Picture Cards**.

Words in Oral Sentences

- Explain that sentences are made up of words.

- Repeat the sentence "I love colors, yes I do!" making a mark on the board for each word. Say the sentence again and ask children to clap for each word. Ask: How many times did you clap? How many words are in the sentence? Count the marks to confirm the answers. Continue with other sentences.

 Getting Ready to Learn

To help children plan their day, tell them that they will–

- listen to a **Big Book**: *I Went Walking*.

- learn the new letters *S* and *s*, and see words that begin with *s*.

- list farm animals in the Science Center.

Big Book

I Went Walking

Selection Summary While talking a walk, a young boy has farm animals of different colors join him.

Key Concepts

Color words

Animal names

English Language Learners

Help children with the sentence *I went walking*, explaining it as: *I went for a walk*. For the clause *looking at me*, restate the phrase as two simple sentences: *I saw a (animal name). The (animal name) was looking at me.*

INSTRUCTION

Reading the Big Book

Building Background

Ask children to remember a walk you've taken together as a class or one they've taken to or from school. Have them tell all the things they saw on the walk. Then introduce the book *I Went Walking* by Sue Williams. Tell children that this book is about a walk, too.

COMPREHENSION STRATEGY
Predict/Infer

Teacher Modeling Model how to predict what the book will be about by previewing the title and the pictures.

> **Think Aloud** Before I read, I can use clues from the title of the story and the pictures to predict what a book is about.

- The title says *I Went Walking* and shows a picture of a boy. When I look at the first few pages, I see that the boy is walking. I also see that a cat has joined him.

- Maybe the boy sees other animals on his walk. Let's read the book and see what happens.

COMPREHENSION SKILL
Sequence of Events

Teacher Modeling Remind children that good readers think about the order in which things happen in a story.

> **Think Aloud** As I read, I'll think about what happens first, next, and last. This will help me remember the story.

Big Book Read Aloud

As you read aloud, emphasize the story sequence with words like *first,*
then, and *next.* Help children discover the next animal by using the
picture clues.

Responding

Oral Language: Personal Response Encourage children to use color
words in their sentences.

- Did you like the story? What was your favorite part?
- Who can name the animals the boy saw? Use the pictures to help you
  remember.
- Did the boy have fun on the walk? How can you tell?

Oral Language: Literature Circle Have children name their favorite
animal in the story. Ask them to share titles of other books they may
have read about farm animals.

Science Center

Materials picture books of farm animals •
drawing paper • crayons . . . .

Place several picture books about
farm animals in the Science
Center. Have children work in
groups of two or three to explore
the books and create a picture list
of farm animals. Children can
refer to the text in the **Big Book**
and in the picture books to label
and draw their lists.

**Extra Support/
Intervention**

Before reading, some children may need
additional help to identify each animal
when previewing the illustrations.

PHONICS

WEEK 1

OBJECTIVES

- Identify words that begin with /s/.
- Identify pictures whose names begin with *s*.
- Form the letters *S, s*.

Materials

- **Alphafriend Card** *Sammy Seal*
- **Letter Card** *s*
- **Picture Cards** *six, sun, sandbox, mat, mop, toast, ten*
- **Blackline Master** 175
- **Phonics Center** Theme 2, Week 1, Day 2

Sammy Seal's Song

(tune: Yankee Doodle)

Sammy Seal will sail the sea
  when summer is the season.

Sammy Seal will sail the sea
  and never need a reason.

Sammy Seal will sail the sea
  in very sunny weather.

Sammy Seal salutes a seagull
  as they sail together!

 Extra Support/ Intervention

To help children remember the sound for *s*, point out that the letter's name gives a clue to its sound: *s*, /s/.

PHONICS
Initial Consonant *s*

❶ Phonemic Awareness Warm-Up

Beginning Sound Read or sing the lyrics to Sammy Seal's song, and have children echo it line-for-line. Have them listen for the /s/ words and "sit" up each time they hear one. See Theme Resources page R2 for music and lyrics.

❷ Teach Phonics

Beginning Letter Display the *Sammy Seal* card, and have children name the letter. This time, Sammy has a letter. What is it? The letter *s* stands for the sound /s/, as in *ssseal*. When you see an *s*, remember *Sammy Seal*. That will help you remember the sound /s/.

Write *seal* on the board, underlining the *s*. What is the first letter in the word *seal*? *Seal* starts with /s/, so *s* is the first letter I write for *seal*.

❸ Guided Practice

Compare *s* and other sounds In a pocket chart, display the *Sammy Seal* card along with **Letter Card** *s*. Place the **Picture Cards** in random order. Children can name a picture, say the beginning sound, and put the card either below the *s* or to the side of the pocket chart. Tell children they will sort more pictures in the **Phonics Center** today.

Handwriting Rhyme: S

S looks like a snake,
curve left then right.
From top to bottom,
makes it right.

Handwriting Rhyme: s

Small s looks like
a snake, too.
Curve left then right,
that's all you do.

Penmanship: Writing S, s Tell children that now they'll learn to write the letters that stand for /s/: capital S and small s. Write each letter as you recite the penmanship rhyme. Children can chant each rhyme as they "write" the letter in the air.

❹ Apply

Have children complete **Practice Book** page 75 at small group time. For additional penmanship practice assign **Blackline Master** 175. Penmanship practice for the continuous stroke style is available on **Blackline Master** 201.

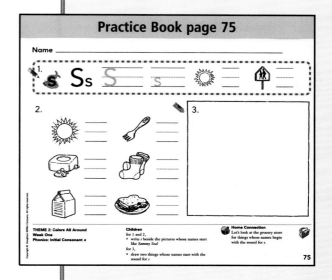

Practice Book page 75

ABC Phonics Center

Materials Phonics Center materials for Theme 2, Week 1, Day 2 ··················

Display Day 2 Direction Chart. Children put *Sammy Seal* (with letter) in one part of Workmat 2. Then they sort remaining pictures by initial letter: *s* or not *s*.

HIGH-FREQUENCY WORD
New Word: *I*

OBJECTIVES

- Read and write the high-frequency word *I*.

Materials

- Word Card *I*
- Picture Cards *cut, hop, run*
- Punctuation Card period
- *Higglety Pigglety: A Book of Rhymes,* page 10

❶ Teach

Introduce the word *I*. Tell children that today they will learn to read and write a word. Explain it's a very important word to know because you use it tell about yourself. Say *I* and use it in context.

I drink milk.　　　*I* like cats.　　　*I* like to sing.

- Write *I* on the board. Point out that it's a letter as well as a word. Ask children to name the letter.

- Explain that the word *I* always uses the capital form. Spell *I* with me, capital *I*.

- Lead children in a chant, clapping on each beat, to help them remember that *I* is spelled capital *I*: capital *I* spells *I*, capital *I* spells *I*.

Word Wall Introduce the Word Wall. Explain that this is where you will put words children will learn to read and write. Post *I*, and tell children to check the Word Wall if they need to remember how to write the word *I*.

❷ Guided Practice

Build these sentences one at a time. In a pocket chart, build rebus sentences. Add the end punctuation and tell children that it marks the end of a sentence.

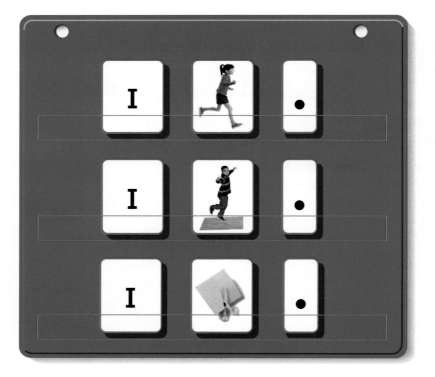

Display *Higglety Pigglety:*
A Book of Rhymes, **page 10.**

- Share the poem "I Love
  Colors" aloud.

- Reread the title of the poem.
  **I'll read the title again. This time
  I'll read it slowly. You listen for
  the word *I*. When you hear it raise
  your hand.**

- Call on children to point to the
  word *I* each time it appears in
  the poem.

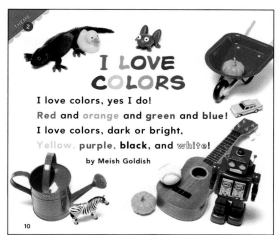

Higglety Pigglety: A Book of Rhymes,
page 10

❸ Apply

- Have children complete **Practice Book** page 76 at small group
  time.

Practice Book page 76

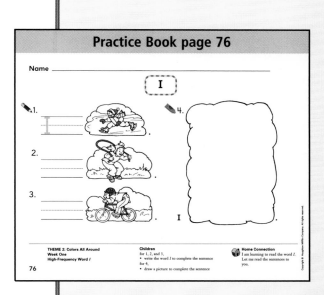

High-Frequency Word   **T39**

OBJECTIVES

- Discuss color words.

Materials

- **Big Book** *I Went Walking*
- ***From Apples to Zebras: A Book of ABC's,*** *page 29*

EXPLORING WORDS
Color Words

Discuss color words.

- Reread a few pages of the **Big Book,** *I Went Walking*. Focus on the color words in an oral context.

- Listen: *I saw a red cow looking at me.* What word tells the color? What else is red? (sample answer: bird) Who can make a sentence just like this about a bird? (I saw a red bird looking at me.)

- Continue with each color mentioned in the book. Children who are able can make their own books based on the pattern of the text. You can record their ideas.

- Have children draw pictures of something colorful. Children who are able can label their pictures with the color word. They can use page 29 of *From Apples to Zebras* as a reference.

VOCABULARY EXPANSION
Using Describing Words

Listening/Speaking/Viewing

Discuss describing words.

- Talk about the colorful animals in *I Went Walking*. Remind children that they can use color to describe things too.
- Page through the story, having children name the animals and their colors. Chart the responses.

Chart additional color words.

- Have children think of other colors that each animal might be. Model creative descriptions using complete sentences.
- List children's suggestions on the chart. Repeat for each animal, prompting children with questions as needed.
- Read the chart aloud. Congratulate children for their good thinking and for all the words they knew to add.

Animal	Color	More Color Words
cat	black	grey, black, spotted, yellow striped
horse	brown	black, white, black spotted

Art Center

Materials drawing paper • crayons or paints

Have children draw pictures of animals they have seen in their neighborhoods. Children can label their drawings with appropriate color words.

OBJECTIVES
- Use color words.
- Use describing words.

Materials
- **Big Book** / *I Went Walking*

Vocabulary Support

The Vocabulary Reader can be used to develop and reinforce vocabulary related to the instruction for this week.

Vocabulary Reader

Colors
by Mary Thurber

DAY 3 week 1

Day at a Glance
T42–T55

Learning to Read

Big Book, *T44*
Phonics: Initial Consonant *s*, *T50*

Word Work

Exploring Words, *T54*

Writing & Oral Language

Shared Writing, *T55*

Daily Routines

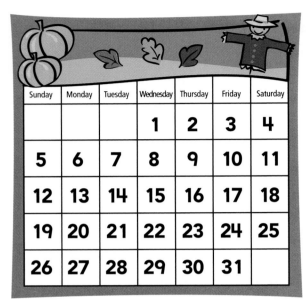

Sunday	Monday	Tuesday	Wednesday	Thursday	Friday	Saturday
			1	2	3	4
5	6	7	8	9	10	11
12	13	14	15	16	17	18
19	20	21	22	23	24	25
26	27	28	29	30	31	

Calendar

Reading the Calendar As you complete your calendar routine, explore the color of the day. Who wore something red today? Who brought in something red? Tell us about it.

Daily Message

Modeled Writing
Include colors and children's names into today's daily message. Children can write their own names or the first letter of their names.

Erica wore a red dress. Miguel and Silvia have red shirts. I have red socks!

Word Wall

Introduce the Word Wall routine. Ask children if they can find the word that they added to the Word Wall yesterday. Call on an individual to point it out. Have children chant the spelling of the word: capital *I* spells *I*.

I

A Word Card for this word appears on page R8.

Daily Phonemic Awareness

Beginning Sounds

- Let's listen for beginning sounds. I will say two words, and you tell me which word begins with Sammy Seal's sound, /s/. Listen: *seven, eight.*

- Say the words with me: *seven, eight.* Which word begins with /s/? . . . Yes, *seven* begins with /s/.

- Continue with the words shown.

sun/me	north/see
fish/seal	dance/sing
sock/mitten	sack/bag
rock/sand	

Words in Oral Sentences

- Remind children that sentences are made up of words. Say Get the red book, making a mark on the board for each word.

- Repeat the sentence and ask children to clap for each word. Ask How many times did you clap? How many words are in the sentence? Count the marks to confirm the answers. Continue with these sentences: *Feed the fish. Eat your snack.*

 Getting Ready to Learn

To help children plan their day, tell them that they will—

- reread and talk about the **Big Book:** *I Went Walking.*

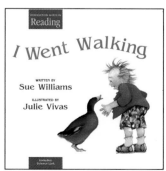

- tell a story called "My Red Boat."

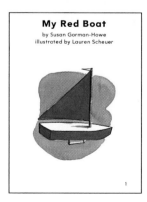

My Red Boat
by Susan Gorman-Howe
illustrated by Lauren Scheuer

- explore favorite colors in the Art Center.

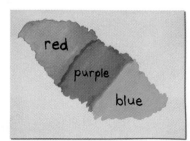

red
purple
blue

Reading the Big Book

Reading for Understanding

Reread the story, emphasizing color words. Children can use the predictability of the text to chime in. Pause for Comprehension points.

I went walking.

What did you see?

2   3

I saw a black cat looking at me.

4   5

I went walking.

What did you see?

6   7

Extra Support/Intervention

Provide additional practice with making predictions. Pause at each page for children to predict what animal the boy will see next.

I saw a brown horse
looking at me.

8

9

I went walking.

What did you see?

10

11

I saw a red cow
looking at me.

12

13

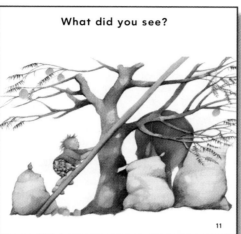

TARGET SKILL

COMPREHENSION STRATEGY

Predict/Infer

pages 2–3

Teacher-Student Modeling Review how you made predictions yesterday before reading the book. Prompts:

- What did the book cover tell us about the story? Did we read about a boy taking a walk? Look at the pictures. How did you guess what the boy would see next?

CRITICAL THINKING

Guiding Comprehension

pages 4–5

- **NOTING DETAILS** Were you right? How did you know the boy would see a cat? (I can see part of the cat in the basket; the basket is now empty; the boy is hugging a black cat.)

TARGET SKILL

COMPREHENSION SKILL

Sequence of Events

pages 8–9

Teacher-Student Modeling Remind children that the events in a story happen in a certain order. This is a good story to figure out what happens next. Who can tell us what animal the boy will see next? I'll ask you to do that as I read.

CRITICAL THINKING

Guiding Comprehension

pages 10–11

- **NOTING DETAILS** What does the boy have to climb to get on the cow?

Reading the Big Book   **T45**

CRITICAL THINKING
Guiding Comprehension

pages 14–15

- **NOTING DETAILS** What animals has the boy seen so far? (a black cat, a brown horse, a red cow)

COMPREHENSION STRATEGY
Predict/Infer

pages 18–19

Student Modeling What animal will the boy see next? How do you know?

REVISITING THE TEXT
Concepts of Print

pages 14–15

Capitalize First Word in Sentence; End Punctuation

- Frame the sentence on page 14. Remind children that the word *I* is always spelled with a capital letter. Tell children that the first word in a sentence also begins with a capital letter. Then point to the end of the sentence. All sentences have end marks. We use a period at the end of a telling sentence. Who will find another period?

I went walking.

What did you see?

14

15

I saw a green duck looking at me.

16

17

I went walking.

What did you see?

18

19

I saw a pink pig looking at me.

20   21

I went walking.   What did you see?

22   23

I saw a yellow dog looking at me.

24   25

Guiding Comprehension

pages 20–21

- **NOTING DETAILS** Is this the same animal you saw on page 19? **How is it different?** (It is cleaner; the boy has washed off the mud.)

pages 24–25

- **NOTING DETAILS** What does the dog do to show he is friendly? Would you like to have a dog like this? Why or why not?

COMPREHENSION SKILL

Sequence of Events

pages 24–25

Student Modeling What will happen next? How do you know?

TARGET SKILL

COMPREHENSION SKILL

Sequence of Events

pages 28–29

Student Modeling How does the story end?

Challenge

Some children will be able to read many words in the story. Others will "pretend read" by using the predictability of the text and the strong language pattern. Let these children read with partners.

Responding

Oral Language: Retelling

Use these prompts to help children retell the story:

- What did the boy do at the beginning of the story?
- What animals did the boy see during his walk?
- How does knowing what will happen next help you to remember the story?
- How was the ending different from the rest of the story?

Oral Language: Literature Circle Have small groups discuss what might happen if the book were to continue. **What other animals might the boy see? What color would these animals be?**

Practice Book Children will complete **Practice Book** page 77 during small group time.

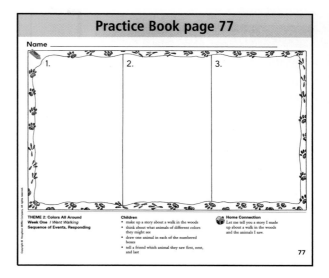

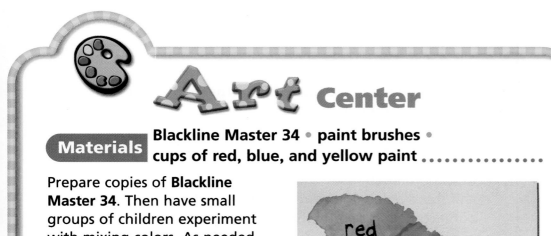

Art Center

Materials | Blackline Master 34 • paint brushes • cups of red, blue, and yellow paint ....

Prepare copies of **Blackline Master 34.** Then have small groups of children experiment with mixing colors. As needed, demonstrate how to mix two paint colors and how to record the results on the record sheets.

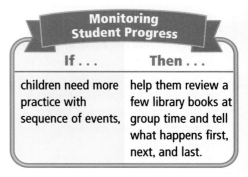

red

purple

blue

Monitoring Student Progress

If . . .	Then . . .
children need more practice with sequence of events,	help them review a few library books at group time and tell what happens first, next, and last.

Responding **T49**

OBJECTIVES

- Identify words that begin with /s/.
- Identify pictures whose names start with the letter *s*.

Materials

- **Alphafriend Card** *Sammy Seal*
- **Alphafriend CD** Theme 2
- **Picture Cards** for *s* and assorted others

PHONICS
Initial Consonant *s*

❶ Phonemic Awareness Warm-Up

Beginning Sound Read the lyrics to Sammy Seal's song aloud, and have children echo it line-for-line. Have them listen for the /s/ words.

- Tell children that you will read the song again slowly. This time, if you hear a word that begins with /s/ raise your hand. If you hear another /s/ word, put your hand down. We'll raise and lower our hands each time we hear an /s/ word. Let's practice with the first line.

- As you say the first line, model raising and lowering your hand alternately for /s/ words. Then say the entire song, having just children raise and lower their hands for /s/ words.

Sammy Seal's Song

(tune: Yankee Doodle)

Sammy Seal will sail the sea
  when summer is the season.

Sammy Seal will sail the sea
  and never need a reason.

Sammy Seal will sail the sea
  in very sunny weather.

Sammy Seal salutes a seagull
  as they sail together!

❷ Teach Phonics

Beginning Letter *s* Display the *Sammy Seal* card and have children name the letter on the picture.

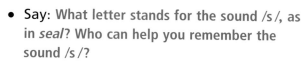

- Say: **What letter stands for the sound /s/, as in *seal*? Who can help you remember the sound /s/?**

- Write *seal* on the board, underlining the *s*. **What is the first letter in the word *seal*? (*s*) *Seal* starts with /s/, so *s* is the first letter I write for *seal*.**

❸ Guided Practice/Apply

- Write *Ss* on the board and circle it. Then write *Ss*, circle it, and draw a line through it to show "not *s*."

- Distribute **Picture Cards** for *s* and assorted others, one per child, to a group of children.

- In turn, children name their picture, say the beginning sound, and stand below the correct symbol on the board. Children without **Picture Cards** verify their decisions.

- Repeat the activity with different groups of children until each child has a chance to name a picture, say the beginning sound, and stand below the correct symbol on the board.

Extra Support/ Intervention

Read "Sing a Song of Sixpence," ***Higglety Pigglety: A Book of Rhymes,*** page 11. Call on volunteers to point to words that begin with /s/ in the tongue twister. Help verify children's choices by reading the words aloud and having children repeat them, listening for the beginning sound.

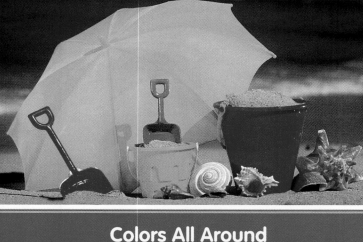

Colors All Around

My Red Boat

by Susan Gorman-Howe
illustrated by Lauren Scheuer

1

PHONICS LIBRARY
Storytelling Practice

Building Background

Let's look at the title page. It says "My Red Boat." What kind of boat is it? Help children identify the cover picture as a sailboat, pointing out the sail. Ask children what things they see on the title page whose names start with /s/. (sailboat, sail)

Preview the pictures on pages 2–3. Have children look quickly to see who the characters are and to predict what the story is about.

2   3

Oral Language

Go back to page 1. Then page through the story and have children help tell what's happening as they carefully view each picture. Use prompts such as these to help children tell the story:

pages 2–3 Whom is this story about? (a boy and his dad) What do
you think they are making? (a sailboat)

page 4 What color sail did the boy and his dad make? (red)

page 5 Where are the boy and his dad now? (at a lake near a play-
ground) Why do you think the boy and his dad have come to the
lake? (to race their sailboat)

pages 6–7 Which sailboat is winning the race? (the boy's red sailboat) How do you know? (The boat is in front of the others.) How
do you think the boy and his dad feel? (happy) How do you know?
(They have their arms in the air as if they are cheering.)

Now have children take turns retelling the story page by page.

Phonics Connection

Now let's go back and look at each page. Raise your hand when you
find something whose name begins with Sammy Seal's sound, /s-s-s/.
(sailboat, sail, spade, saw, screwdriver, skate, scissors, soccer
ball, string, spider, soap, sink, stool, stapler, swings, slide,
squirrel, stroller, sun, swans)

Home Connection

Children can color the pictures whose
names begin with /s/ in the take-home version
of "My Red Boat." After retelling on Day 4,
they can take it home to share with family
members. (See **Phonics Library Blackline
Masters.**)

4

Race at 6:00

5

6

7

OBJECTIVES

- Explore color words.

Materials

- *From Apples to Zebras: A Book of ABC's,* page 29

EXPLORING WORDS
Color Words

Create a color chart.

- Display page 29 of *From Apples to Zebras: A Book of ABC's.* Remind children that they have been talking about colors. Call on children to point to and name the colors on the page.

- Discuss with children how color words help them describe what something looks like.

- Make a color chart for the Writing Center like the one on page 29 of *From Apples to Zebras.* Begin by listing the featured color words on the left side of the chart. If possible, use the appropriate color marker for each color word.

- Have children brainstorm items for each color. Record their suggestions with simple line drawings that children can then color in.

Have children choose a favorite color, and draw their own set of items for the color. Allow time for children to share their drawings with the class.

COLORS		
red	🍎	STOP
yellow	☀	🍌
blue	🐦	🍇
orange	🎃	
green	🐸	

SHARED WRITING
Writing a Description

Take an observations walk.

- Display the illustrations in *I Went Walking* and have children retell the story in their own words using complete sentences.

- Tell children that they will write their own *I Went Walking* story. Take children on a brief walk around the school or the school grounds. As you walk, point out the colors of different objects.

Create an observations chart together.

- When you return to the classroom, ask children to share their observations. Record all suggestions on chart paper.

OBJECTIVES
- Use color words to describe objects.

Materials
- **Big Book** / *Went Walking*

DAY **3**

WRITING

WEEK 1

English Language Learners

Invite children to create a "Book of New Words," where they can draw pictures of words they have learned during this theme. Help children add color or other describing words.

Day at a Glance
T56–T63

Learning to Read

Big Book, *T58*
Phonics: Review Initial Consonant *s, T60*

Word Work

Exploring Words, *T62*

Writing & Oral Language

Interactive Writing, *T63*

Daily Routines

Sunday	Monday	Tuesday	Wednesday	Thursday	Friday	Saturday
			1	2	3	4
5	6	7	8	9	10	11
12	13	14	15	16	17	18
19	20	21	22	23	24	25
26	27	28	29	30	31	

Calendar

Reading the Calendar Talk about today's color as you complete the calendar routine. Encourage children to describe the colors they've worn. Be sure to share your own contribution too.

Daily Message

Modeled Writing
Use some words that begin with *s* in today's message. Have a child circle each *s* at the beginning of a word.

Sal has on brown socks today.

Word Wall

Call on a child to point out the word *I* on the Word Wall. Have children chant the spelling of the word: capital *I* spells *I*.

I

A Word Card for this word appears on page R8.

Daily Phonemic Awareness

Beginning Sounds

- Listen: *pig, pink*. Say the words with me: *pig, pink*. Do you hear the same sound at the beginning of each word? Yes, *pig* and *pink* begin with the same sound. Help children isolate the beginning sound, /p/.

- Play Same Sound Sort. I'll say two words. If they begin with the same sound, raise your hand. If they do not, cover your ears. Help children isolate each beginning sound to verify their decisions.

| duck/doll | rake/hat | bird/bat |
| cat/dog | leaf/lion | soap/sun |

Words in Oral Sentences

- Remind children that words are made up of sounds and that sentences are made up of words.

- Listen to my sentence: *The cat sat.* Listen again and clap for each word. How many words did you hear?

- Repeat with *The white cat sat on the chair.*

Getting Ready to Learn

To help children plan their day, tell them that they will—

- read the Science Link: *What's My Favorite Color?*

- sort pictures in the **Phonics Center**.

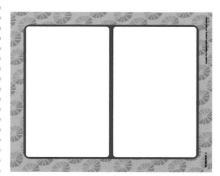

- retell a story called "My Red Boat."

My Red Boat
by Susan Gorman-Howe
illustrated by Lauren Scheuer

OBJECTIVES

- Identify sequence.
- Recognize use of capital letter at the beginning of a sentence.
- Recognize use of end punctuation: period, question mark.

READING THE BIG BOOK
Science Link

Building Background

Ask children to name their favorite fruit. Read aloud the title of the selection and discuss the photograph. Invite children to name the fruits and describe their colors.

Reading for Understanding Pause for discussion as you share the selection.

 COMPREHENSION STRATEGY
Predict/Infer

Student Modeling Point out to children that the title asks a question, *What's My Favorite Color?,* and that the selection shows different kinds of fruit. Cover page 35 and then read aloud page 34. What does this page show? The author says she likes yellow, but that she likes green more. What do you think the next page will show? What clues help you to know that? Uncover and read page 35 to confirm children's predictions.

 Extra Support/ Intervention

Some children may not be familiar with all the different fruits shown in the article. Prior to reading, children may benefit from describing and tasting actual fruits or looking at fruits in other books.

English Language Learners

Before working with the selection, review or introduce fruit names. Then have children classify fruits according to color, taste, or shape.

Challenge

Prepare cards for the words and end marks for several sentences from the selection. One child can build a sentence and a partner can find it in the book.

 COMPREHENSION SKILL
Sequence of Events

Student Modeling Tell children that sometimes authors give clues about what will be shown next. What does the author say on page 34 that helps you know what fruit will be shown on the next page?

These bananas are yellow.
I like yellow, but I like green more.

34

These pears are green.
I like green, but I like orange more.

35

34　　　　　　　　　　　　　　　　**35**

These oranges are orange.
I like orange, but I like red more.

36

These cherries are red.
Red is my favorite color because...

37

36　　　　　　　　　　　　　　　　**37**

cherries are my favorite fruit!
What color is your favorite fruit?

38

38

COMPREHENSION STRATEGY
Predict/Infer

page 36

- Cover page 37 and then read aloud page 36. Say: The author likes orange, but she says she likes red more. What do you think the next page will show? Why do you say that?

CRITICAL THINKING
Guiding Comprehension

page 37

- **COMPARE AND CONTRAST** What other fruits can you name that are red? Which of these fruits do you like best? Why?

REVISITING THE TEXT
Concepts of Print

pages 37–38

Capitalize First Word in Sentence; End Punctuation

- Frame and read: *These cherries are red.* Why does *These* begin with a capital letter?

- Recall that all sentences end with a mark. The sentence (*These cherries are red.*) is a telling sentence so it ends with a period.

- Frame the second sentence on page 38 and read it aloud. This sentence asks a question. What mark do we use at the end of a sentence that asks a question?

Responding

Oral Language: Summarizing Have children summarize the selection, using the pictures as prompts.

OBJECTIVES

- Identify words that begin with /s/.
- Identify pictures whose names start with the letter *s*.

Materials

- *From Apples to Zebras: A Book of ABC's,* page 20
- Alphafriend Card *Sammy Seal*
- Alphafolder *Sammy Seal*
- Letter Card *s*
- Picture Cards *bug, map, red, sad, salt, sandals, six, ten*
- Phonics Center Theme 2, Week 1, Day 4

PHONICS
Review Initial Consonant *s*

Review Phonemic Awareness: Beginning Sound Display the scene in Sammy Seal's Alphafolder.

- One thing I see in the picture is the sun. Say *sun* with me. Does *sun* begin with the same sound as Sammy Seal, /s/?

- Call on children to point to and name other items in the picture that begin with /s/.

Review consonant *s* Using self-stick notes, cover the words on page 20 of *From Apples to Zebras: A Book of ABC's.* Then display the page.

Ss

seal

salt

salad

sandwich

20

From Apples to Zebras: A Book of ABC's, page 20

- Ask children what letter they expect to see at the beginning of each word and why. Uncover the words so that children can check their predictions.

- Provide each child with a self-stick note. Ask children to write the letter *s* on their notes.

- Have children place their notes on objects in the classroom that begin with /s/. Allow children to mark the same item.

- Confirm children's decisions by listing the words for the items they marked on chart paper. Call on children to underline the *s* in each word you write.

<u>s</u>ink   <u>s</u>oap

<u>s</u>and table

<u>S</u>cience Corner

<u>s</u>ock puppet

 Home Connection

Ask children to look at home for items or for names that begin with the letter *s*. Children can draw pictures to show what they have found.

Practice/Apply In a pocket chart, display the card for *Sammy Seal* and the **Letter Card** *s*.

- Hold up **Picture Cards** one at a time. Children signal "thumbs up" for a word whose name starts with Sammy Seal's sound, /s/. Repeat the word, emphasizing initial /s/ as you place the picture under the letter *s*. Children signal "thumbs down" for pictures that do not begin with /s/.

Pictures: *sandals, map, ten, six, red, sad, bug, salt*

- Tell children they will sort more pictures in the **Phonics Center** today.

- Have children complete **Practice Book** page 78 at small group time.

- In groups today, children will also identify pictures whose names begin with initial *s* as they retell the **Phonics Library** story "My Red Boat." See suggestions, pages T51–T53.

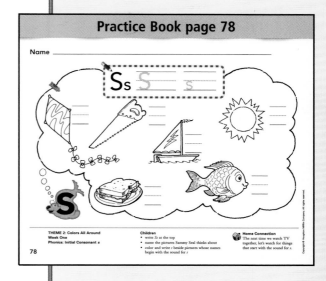

Practice Book page 78

Name _____

THEME 2: Colors All Around
Week One
Phonics: Initial Consonant *s*

78

Children
• write *Ss* at the top
• name the pictures Sammy Seal thinks about
• color and write *s* beside pictures whose names begin with the sound for *s*

Home Connection The next time we watch TV together, let's watch for things that start with the sound for *s*.

Phonics Center

Materials Phonics Center materials for Theme 2, Week 1, Day 4 ·

Display Day 4 Direction Chart. Children put **Letter Card** *s* in one part of Workmat 2. Then they sort remaining pictures by initial letter: *s* and not *s*.

Monitoring Student Progress

If . . .	Then . . .
children have trouble identifying /s/ words,	have them work with you or a partner to name items in the **Alphafolder** scene.

OBJECTIVES

● Explore color words.

Materials

● **Big Book** *What's My Favorite Color?*

EXPLORING WORDS
Color Words

Make a chart of food colors together.

● Display the chart children used during yesterday's Exploring Words activity. (See page T54.) Read the chart with children, emphasizing the color words.

● Recall that in *What's My Favorite Color?* the author named different fruits that are usually known for being certain colors.

● As children brainstorm other foods that are the same colors, create a chart.

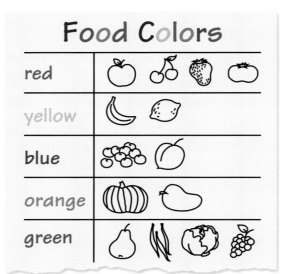

INTERACTIVE WRITING
Writing a Description

OBJECTIVES
- Participate in interactive writing.
- Use color words in an oral context.

Materials
- Big Book *I Went Walking*

Prepare to write a description together.

- Share pages 2–5 of *I Went Walking*. Have children use color words to describe what they see.

- Display the chart from yesterday's Shared Writing. Review what children saw on their walk. Tell children that they will write a class story using the pattern in *I Went Walking*.

Write a description together.

- Write the following sentences on chart paper: *I went walking. What did you see? I saw a _____* .

- Model how to complete the sentence, using an item from the walk. Then read the sentences, adding the item you chose.

- Continue writing the class story, having the children contribute their ideas. Share the pen by having children add punctuation and write *I* or the initial letter *s*.

Writing Center

Materials Blackline Master 35

Place copies of **Blackline Master** 35, the *Our Class Walk* chart, and the *I Went Walking* story in the Writing Center. Children can draw a picture or write the words to complete **Blackline Master** 35. Some children may wish to make their own books.

DAY 5
week 1

Day at a Glance
T64–T71

Learning to Read

Revisiting the Literature, *T66*
Phonics Review: Consonant *s,*
T68

Word Work

Exploring Words, *T70*

Writing & Oral Language

Independent Writing, *T71*

Daily Routines

Sunday	Monday	Tuesday	Wednesday	Thursday	Friday	Saturday
			1	2	3	4
5	6	7	8	9	10	11
12	13	14	15	16	17	18
19	20	21	22	23	24	25
26	27	28	29	30	31	

Calendar

Reading the Calendar Use the color of the day to mark the calendar and launch children into sharing the colored items they've worn or brought in. Make children aware of shades of color. Tula's rubber duck is a bright yellow, like the sun. Mark's shirt is a golden yellow, like honey.

Daily Message

Modeled Writing As you write the daily message, call on children to help you. What kind of letter should I use to begin my sentence? Is this a telling or asking sentence? Should I put a period or a question mark at the end?

Today we go to the library. How many books do you think you will borrow?

Word Wall

Share this riddle with children. I am a letter, but I am also a word. I am always spelled with a capital. Who am I? When children guess *I,* have one of them point to *I* on the Word Wall.

I

A Word Card for this word appears on page R8.

Daily Phonemic Awareness

Beginning Sounds

- Play a guessing game to call attention to the beginning sounds in names. Choose a name that begins with /s/. I am thinking of someone's name in this room. The name starts with /s/. Who has a name that starts with /s/?

- Allow children to guess all the possibilities before revealing the name you had in mind. Repeat several times until children have guessed all of the /s/ names.

Words in Oral Sentences

- Listen to this sentence: *I like to draw.* Now clap for each word as I say it again. How many words did you hear?

- Try another one: *The sun is yellow.* If children clap twice for *yellow,* explain that one word like *yellow* can have two parts. Give another example like *Matthew* or *Caitlin.*

To help children plan their day, tell them that they will–

- reread and talk about all the books they've read this week.

- take home a story they can share.

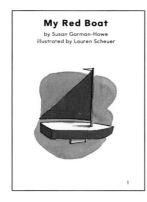

My Red Boat
by Susan Gorman-Howe
illustrated by Lauren Scheuer

- write about their favorite foods in their journals.

José

● Review the week's selections.

REVISITING THE LITERATURE
Literature Discussion

Review the week's selections, using these suggestions.

● Have children tell why the boy in *I Need a Lunch Box* wanted a lunch box. Ask what was unusual about the boy's dream.

● Ask children to recall the animals the boy in *I Went Walking* saw on his walk.

● Have children recall *What's My Favorite Color?* Select children to find their favorite fruits and colors in the selection.

● Together retell the story "My Red Boat." Ask individuals to name the /s/ objects in the story.

● Ask children to vote for their favorite book of the week, and then read the winner aloud.

COMPREHENSION SKILL
Sequence of Events

Compare Books Remind children that knowing the order in which things happen can help them to better understand and enjoy a story.

● Browse through each selection, inviting comments about how children used the sequence of events to help them make predictions.

● After looking at each story, help children develop a one- or two-sentence summary.

PRACTICE

BUILDING FLUENCY
Storytelling

Revisit Familiar Texts Review the **Phonics Library** story "My Red Boat." Remind children that they've learned the sound for *s*, /s/. As children retell the **Phonics Library** story "My Red Boat," have them look for pictures whose names begin with /s/.

Review Feature several familiar **Phonics Library** titles in the Book Corner. Have children demonstrate their growing skills by choosing one to describe the pictures, alternating pages with a partner. Remind them to speak in complete sentences.

Oral Language Frequent retellings of familiar texts help children develop their vocabulary. Model how to describe an illustration expressively. Then have children try it.

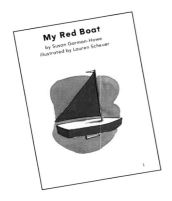

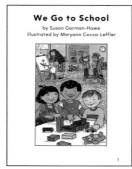

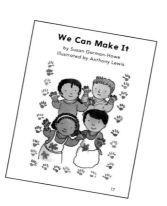

Books for Small-Group Reading

The materials listed below provide reading practice for children at different levels.

Leveled Reader

Little Big Book

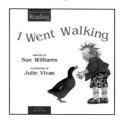

Little Readers for Guided Reading

Houghton Mifflin Classroom Bookshelf

Home Connection

Remind children to share the take-home version of "My Red Boat" with their families.

OBJECTIVES

- Review initial consonant *s*.
- Review letter names.
- Make sentences with high-frequency word *I*.

Materials

- **Word Card** *I*
- **Punctuation Card** *period*
- **Picture Cards** for *s* and assorted others; *cut, dig, hop, hug, run*

PHONICS
Initial Consonant: *s*

TARGET SKILL

❶ Review

Review identifying initial consonant s. Tell children that they will take turns naming pictures that begin with /s/ and writing the letter that stands for /s/.

- Place two **Picture Cards,** one for *s* and one distractor, along the chalkboard ledge.

- Choose a child to name each picture, and write *s* above the /s/ picture. Then have the rest of the class verify that *s* has been written above the correct picture.

- Write the picture name on the board. Choose another child to underline the initial consonant *s*.

- Continue until everyone has a chance to write or underline *s*.

Review letter names. Recite the alphabet together with the children. Hold up **Letter Cards** at random and have children name them.

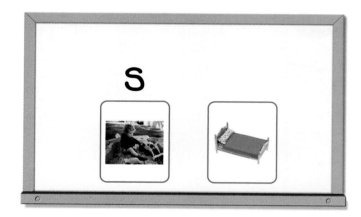

HIGH-FREQUENCY WORD

I

❷ Review

Review the high-frequency word *I*.

- Give each small group the **Word Cards, Picture Cards,** and **Punctuation Card** needed to make a sentence. Each child holds one card.

- Children stand and arrange themselves to make a sentence for others to read.

❸ Practice/Apply

- Children can complete **Practice Book** page 79 independently and read it to you during small group time.

- Pass out copies of **Practice Book** pages 193–194, *I* . Read the title aloud.

- Ask children to tell who is speaking. Point to the girl and tell children that she is telling the story.

- For each page, have children look at the picture and tell what the girl is doing. Have them read the page silently.

- Ask a child to read the page aloud. Use questions such as the following to prompt discussion:

   Pages 1–3 What does the girl do in the water? What does she do in the sand?

   Page 4 Why do you think the girl fell asleep? What would you like best about a day at the beach?

- Then have children count the number of times the word *I* is used in the story.

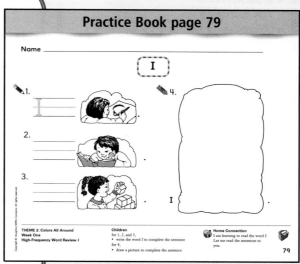

Practice Book page 79

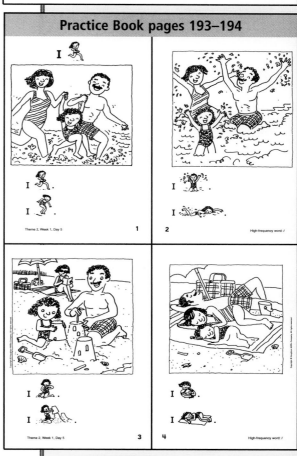

Practice Book pages 193–194

Monitoring Student Progress

If . . .	Then . . .
children need help remembering the sound for consonant *s*,	have them listen to Sammy Seal's song and listen for *s* words.

OBJECTIVES

● Explore color words.

Materials

● *From Apples to Zebras: A Book of ABC's,* page 29
● Photograph or teacher-made picture of a rainbow

EXPLORING WORDS
Color Words

Discuss and identify colors of the sky.

● Display page 29 of *From Apples to Zebras: A Book of ABC's.* Call on children to point to and name the colors on the page.

● Then ask children what colors they see when they look at the sky. What color is the daytime sky? the nighttime sky? What color is the sun? the moon? the stars? Have you ever looked at the sky and seen lots of different colors? What colors did you see?

● If children do not mention a rainbow in the discussion, encourage children who have seen rainbows to tell about them.

● Display a photograph or a picture of a rainbow and have children name the colors in the rainbow.

● Have children draw or paint their own rainbows. They can label the colors in their rainbows by referring to the class color chart or page 29 of *From Apples to Zebras: A Book of ABC's.*

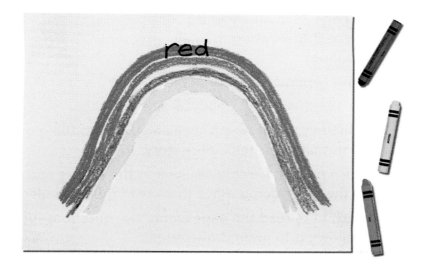

INDEPENDENT WRITING
Journals

OBJECTIVES
● Write independently.

Materials
● journals

Preparing to Write

● Review the charts from this week's Shared and Interactive Writing activities. (See pages T55 and T63.)

● Ask children to point out the color words.

Writing Independently

● Distribute the journals, and tell children that today's journal entry will be about their favorite color.

● Tell children that they can use the Word Wall, the story charts, and the color word lists to help them write words. Remind them to write from left to right.

● Invite children to share their journals in small groups.

Portfolio Opportunity

Mark journal entries you would like to share with parents. Allow children to indicate their best efforts or favorite works for sharing as well.

LEVELED READERS

WEEK 1

Things I See

Summary: *This nonfiction book describes a variety of things seen in the natural world, including a bug, bird, flower, grass, tree, pumpkin, and the sky.*

Story Words

the *p. 2*

see *p. 2*

High-Frequency Word

New Word

I *p. 2*

▲ ON LEVEL

Building Background and Vocabulary

Introduce this story by telling children that this book is about things we can see outside in the world of nature. Preview the photographs with children. Encourage them to share their own experiences looking at things in the natural world. Ask children to help you make a list of things, such as birds and bugs, that they have seen in the world of nature.

Comprehension Skill: Sequence of Events

Read together the Strategy Focus on the book flap. Then remind children, as they read, to think about which pictures they see first, next, and last.

Responding

Discussing the Book Ask children to share their personal responses to the book. Begin by asking them to talk about what they liked best about the book or what they found the most interesting. Have children point to sentences or photographs they especially enjoyed. Ask children if they have seen each of the things pictured in the story. When do they get a chance to spend time outside? What things do they like to look for in the world of nature? Why?

Responding Work with children to answer the questions on the inside back cover. Then encourage them to complete the Writing and Drawing activity. Have children take turns explaining their drawings to the class. Display the pictures on a bulletin board titled *Things We Can See Outside*.

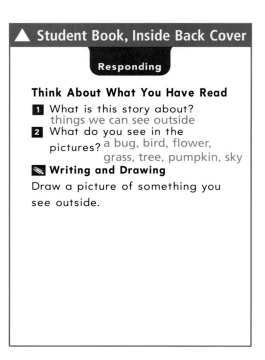

▲ Student Book, Inside Back Cover

Responding

Think About What You Have Read

1 What is this story about?
  things we can see outside
2 What do you see in the
  pictures? a bug, bird, flower,
              grass, tree, pumpkin, sky

Writing and Drawing

Draw a picture of something you see outside.

Building Fluency

Model Have children follow along as you reread pages 2 and 3 to them. Point out that the first three words, *I see the,* on the two pages are the same. Tell children that these words begin every page in the book.

Practice Divide the group into two smaller groups and continue reading the book aloud. For each page, have one group read the repeating phrase, *I see the*, while the other group reads the word that tells the item seen in the picture. Then ask children to retell the story in their own words.

Oral Language Development

Color Words Discuss color words with children. Explain that color words are words that tell the color of things. Have children page through the book with you. For each photograph, ask volunteers to name the color of the thing shown in the picture (*red, black, and yellow bug, yellow bird, purple flower, green grass, red tree, orange pumpkin, blue sky*).

Practice Reread the book with children and review the color words to describe each photograph. Have children practice using the color words by naming other things that are the same color as the things shown in the photographs.

High-Frequency Word
New Word: *I*

Display the Word Card for *I*. Read the word aloud. Ask children to listen for the word as you read page 2 in *Things I See*. Then have them turn to page 4 in the story. Review the Word Card and ask children to point to the word *I* in the text. Ask children to read the sentence on the page together. Then have children point out the word *I* on the remaining pages of the book.

I

Lesson Overview

Literature

HOUGHTON MIFFLIN
Reading

In the Big Blue Sea

by Chyng Feng Sun
Photography by Norbert Wu

Includes:
Science Link

Selection Summary

In this photo essay, children are invited to accompany Norbert Wu as he photographs colorful fish in the ocean.

❶ Teacher Read Aloud
- *Caps of Many Colors*

❷ Big Book
- *In the Big Blue Sea*
Genre: Nonfction

❸ Wordless Book
Phonics Library
- "Look at Me!"

Look at Me!
by Susan Gorman-Howe
illustrated by Jennifer Plecas
FACE PAINTING

❹ Science Link

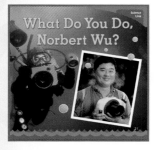

What Do You Do, Norbert Wu?

This Link appears after the main Big Book selection.

Leveled Books

Vocabulary Reader

- Below Level, ELL
- Lesson

Leveled Reader

- On Level, Above Level
- Lesson
- Take-Home Version

Plus!
Online Leveled Books

Instructional Support

Planning and Practice

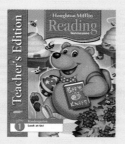

Tennessee Teacher's Edition

Teacher's Resources

Alphafriends

Practice book

Differentiated Instruction

Intervention/Extra Support

English Language Learners

Challenge

Ready-Made Centers

Phonics Center

Building Vocabulary

Reading in Science and Social Studies
- 30 books and activities
- support for Tennessee content standards

Hands-On Literacy Centers for Week 2
- activities
- manipulatives
- routines

Technology

Audio Selection
In the Big Blue Sea

www.eduplace.com
- over 1,000 Online Leveled Books

Daily Lesson Plans

 Technology
Lesson Planner CD-ROM allows you to customize the chart below to develop your own lesson plans.

T Skill tested on Weekly or Theme Skills Test and/or Integrated Theme Test

 Tennessee Curriculum Standards indicated in blue.

WEEK 2   **DAILY LESSON PLANS**

60–90 minutes

Learning to Read

Phonemic Awareness

Phonics

High–Frequency Words

Comprehension

Concepts of Print

Vocabulary Reader

Look at Me!

Leveled Reader

DAY 1

K.1.01.e, K.1.06.a
Daily Routines, *T80–T81*
Calendar, Message, High-Frequency Words

 Phonemic Awareness **T** K.1.04.f, K.1.04.g

Teacher Read Aloud, *T82–T85*

Comprehension Strategy, *T82* K.1.09.b.2
Summarize

Comprehension Skill, *T82* K.1.08.c
Inferences: Making Predictions **T**

Phonemic Awareness, *T86–T87* K.1.04.f
Beginning Sound /m/ **T**

Cross-Curricular Activity, T79 SC.K.5.2

Leveled Reader
K.1.06, K.1.07, K.1.09.a

DAY 2

K.1.01.g, K.3.02.e, K.1.06.a
Daily Routines, *T90–T91*
Calendar, Message, High-Frequency Words

Phonemic Awareness **T** K.1.04.f, K.1.04.g

Reading the Big Book, *T92–T93*

Comprehension Strategy, *T92* K.1.09.b.2
Summarize

Comprehension Skill, *T92* K.1.08.c
Inferences: Making Predictions

Phonics, *T94–T95* K.1.04.f
Initial Consonant *m* **T**

High-Frequency Word, *T96–T97* K.1.06.a
New Word: *see* **T**

Word and Picture Book, *T97*
K.1.01.e, K.1.13.a, K.1.12.a

Leveled Reader
K.1.06, K.1.07, K.1.09.a

30–45 minutes

Word Work

High-Frequency Word Practice

Exploring Words

High-Frequency Word Practice, *T88* K.1.06.a
Word: *I*

High-Frequency Word Practice, *T98* K.3.02, K.2.10.c
Building Sentences

30–45 minutes

Writing and Oral Language

Vocabulary

Writing

Listening/Speaking/Viewing

Oral Language: Vocabulary, *T89* K.1.01.a
Exact Naming Words

Vocabulary Reader K.1.07.a

Vocabulary Reader K.1.07.a

Vocabulary Expansion, *T99* K.1.01.a
Exact Naming Words

Listening/Speaking/Viewing, *T99*
K.3.04, K.2.02.a

 Half-Day Kindergarten

Focus on lessons for tested skills marked with **T**. Then choose other activities as time allows.

Target Skills of the Week

Phonemic Awareness	Beginning Sounds; Words in Oral Sentences
Phonics	Initial Consonant: *Mm*
Comprehension	Inferences: Making Predictions; Summarize
Vocabulary	High-Frequency; Color Words; Exact Naming Words
Fluency	Phonics Library

DAY 3

K.1.01.e, K.1.06.a

Daily Routines, *T100–T101*
Calendar, Message, High-Frequency Words

Phonemic Awareness K.1.04.f, K.1.04.g

Reading the Big Book, *T102–T107*

Comprehension Strategy, *T103, T104*
Summarize K.1.09.b.2

Comprehension Skill, *T103, T105* K.1.08.c
Inferences: Making Predictions **T**

Concepts of Print, *T104* K.3.02.d, K.3.02.e
Capitalize First Word in Sentence; End Punctuation **T**

Phonics, *T108* K.1.04.f
Initial Consonant *m* **T**

Storytelling Practice, *T109–T111*
"Look at Me!" K.1.13.a, K.1.04.f, K.1.08.c, K.1.08.d, K.1.01.h

Vocabulary Reader K.1.07.a

Leveled Reader
K.1.06, K.1.07, K.1.09.a

Exploring Words, *T112*
Color Words K.1.07.a, K.1.01.e, K.2.01.a

Shared Writing, *T113* K.2.02.b, K.2.07.b, K.2.03.d
Writing a Description

DAY 4

K.1.01.g, K.1.04.f, K.1.06.a

Daily Routines, *T114–T115*
Calendar, Message, High-Frequency Words

Phonemic Awareness T K.1.04.f, K.1.04.g

Reading the Science Link, *T116–T117*

Comprehension Strategy, *T116*
Summarize K.1.09.b.2

Comprehension Skill, *T116* K.1.08.c
Inferences: Making Predictions **T**

Concepts of Print, *T117* K.3.02.d, K.3.02.e
Capitalize First Word in Sentence; End Punctuation **T**

Phonics, *T118–T119* K.1.04.f
Initial Consonant *m* **T**

Vocabulary Reader K.1.07.a

Leveled Reader
K.1.06, K.1.07, K.1.09.a

Exploring Words, *T120*
Color Words K.1.07.a, K.2.01.a, K.2.01.c

Interactive Writing, *T121*
Writing a Description K.2.02.b, K.2.03.c, K.2.03.d

DAY 5

K.1.01.e, K.3.02.d, K.3.02.e, K.1.06.a

Daily Routines,
T122–T123 Calendar, Message, High-Frequency Words

Phonemic Awareness T K.1.04.f, K.1.04.g

Revisiting the Literature, *T124*
K.1.09.2, K.1.14.c, K.1.01.g

Comprehension Skill, *T124* K.1.08.c
Inferences: Making Predictions **T**

Storytelling, *T125* K.1.01.h, K.1.06.c

Phonics Review, *T126* K.1.04.f
Initial Consonant *m, s* **T**

High-Frequency Word Review, *T127* K.1.06.a
Words: *I, see* **T**

Word and Picture Book, *T127*
K.1.01.e, K.1.13.a, K.1.12.a

Vocabulary Reader K.1.07.a

Leveled Reader
K.1.06, K.1.07, K.1.09.a

Exploring Words, *T128* K.3.01.b, K.1.01.f
Color Words

Independent Writing, *T129* K.2.11.a
Journals

Concepts of Print lessons teach important foundational skills for Phonics.

Managing Flexible Groups

Leveled Instruction and Leveled Practice

	DAY 1	**DAY 2**
WHOLE CLASS	• Daily Routines (TE pp. T80–T81) • Teacher Read Aloud: *Caps of Many Colors* (TE pp. T82–T85) • Phonemic Awareness lesson (TE pp. T86–T87)	• Daily Routines (TE pp. T90–T91) • Big Book: *In the Big Blue Sea* (TE pp. T92–T93) • Phonics lesson (TE pp. T94–T95) • High-Frequency Word lesson (TE pp. T96–T97)
SMALL GROUPS *Organize small groups according to children's needs.*	**TEACHER-LED GROUPS** • Begin Practice Book pp. 81, 82, 83, 84. (TE pp. T83, T87) • Introduce Phonics Center. (TE p. T87) • Leveled Reader	**TEACHER-LED GROUPS** • Begin Practice Book pp. 85, 86. (TE pp. T95, T97) • Write letters *M, m;* begin handwriting Blackline Master 169 or 195. (TE p. T95) • Introduce Phonics Center. (TE p. T95) • Leveled Reader • Vocabulary Reader
	INDEPENDENT GROUPS • Complete Practice Book pp. 81, 82, 83, 84. (TE pp. T83, T87) • Use Phonics Center. (TE p. T87)	**INDEPENDENT GROUPS** • Complete Practice Book pp. 85, 86. (TE pp. T95, T97) • Complete Blackline Master 169 or 195. • Use Phonics Center. (TE p. T95) • **Fluency Practice** Reread Word and Picture Book *I See.* (Practice Book pp. 195–196)

English Language Learners Support is provided in the Reaching All Learners notes throughout the week.

Independent Activities

• Complete Practice Book pages 81–89.
• Complete penmanship practice (Teacher's Resource Blackline Master 169 or 195).
• Retell familiar Phonics Library stories or reread Word and Picture book stories.
• Share trade books from Leveled Bibliography. (See pp. T4–T5)

DAY 3

- Daily Routines (TE pp. T100–T101)
- Big Book: *In the Big Blue Sea* (TE pp. T102–T107)
- Phonics lesson (TE p. T108)

TEACHER-LED GROUPS

- Begin Practice Book p. 87. (TE p. T106)
- Tell the Phonics Library story: "Look at Me!" (TE pp. T109–T111)
- Leveled Reader
- Vocabulary Reader

INDEPENDENT GROUPS

- Complete Practice Book p. 87. (TE p. T106)
- **Fluency Practice** Retell Phonics Library: "Look at Me!" (TE pp. T109–T111)

DAY 4

- Daily Routines (TE pp. T114–T115)
- Science Link: *What Do You Do, Norbert Wu?* (TE pp. T116–T117)
- Phonics lesson (TE pp. T118–T119)

TEACHER-LED GROUPS

- Begin Practice Book p. 88. (TE p. T119)
- Introduce the Phonics Center. (TE p. T119)
- **Fluency Practice** Reread Word and Picture Book *I See*.
- Leveled Reader
- Vocabulary Reader

INDEPENDENT GROUPS

- Complete Practice Book p. 88. (TE p. T119)
- **Fluency Practice** Color and retell Phonics Library: "Look at Me!" (TE pp. T109–T111)
- Use Phonics Center. (TE p. T119)

DAY 5

- Daily Routines (TE pp. T122–T123)
- Retelling (TE pp. T124–T125)
- Phonics and High-Frequency Word Review (TE pp. T126–T127)

TEACHER-LED GROUPS

- Read Word and Picture Book: *I See* .
- Begin Practice Book p. 89. (TE p. T127)
- **Fluency Practice** Retell the Take-Home version of "Look at Me!"
- Leveled Reader
- Vocabulary Reader

INDEPENDENT GROUPS

- Complete Practice Book p. 89. (TE p. T127)
- **Fluency Practice** Reread Word and Picture Book: *I See* . Retell a favorite Phonics Library or Leveled Reader story.

- Retell or reread Little Big Books.
- Listen to Big Book Audio CDs.
- Use the Phonics Center and other Centers. (See pp. T78–T79)

Turn the page for more independent activities.

Ready-Made for Tennessee

Independent Activities

Building Vocabulary

ELA.K.1.01.a, ELA.K.1.01.e,
ELA.K.1.01.f, ELA.K.1.01.g,
ELA.K.1.07.a, ELA.K.1.07.b

Center Activity 5

Building Vocabulary
Center Activity 5
In the Big Blue Sea

2 Learn from Context — Small Groups | Connect to Science

Underwater Adventure!
Did you ever wonder what it is like to dive into the sea? Take a look!

bubbles · surface · tank · mask · fin

1 Read the Words

Vocabulary Link
dive

New Words

tank a thing that holds air

bubbles little bits of air in water

mask something that covers your face to keep out water

surface the top of the water

fin part of a fish that helps it swim and turn

3 Do an Activity

Leveled Activities on back of card
● Below Level
▲ On Level
■ Above Level

Hands-On Literacy Centers
In the Big Blue Sea

Challenge and Routine Cards

Buddy Reading
① Get a buddy.
② Read a book.
③ Talk.
Share Draw.

1. Underwater Scene
Planning the Scene
· Think about the fish you want to draw.
· Think of other sea animals and plants.

TIPS
· Fill the page with your picture.
· Press hard with your crayons.

Making the Poster
· ___ the scene.
· Label your poster.
· Paint over your picture with blue paint.

Sharing the Poster
Tell the class about your poster.

Manipulatives

see

Reading in Science

Independent Book
Our Home Is the Pond
Students apply comprehension skills to fiction text.

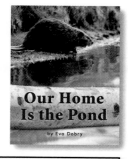

Our Home Is the Pond
by Eva Dobry

SC.K.5.2, ELA.K.1.09.b.2

Center Activity 5

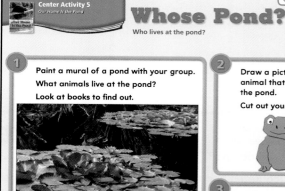

Reading in Science
Center Activity 5
Our Home Is the Pond

Small Groups

Whose Pond?
Who lives at the pond?

1 Paint a mural of a pond with your group. What animals live at the pond? Look at books to find out.

Ducks live in a pond.

2 Draw a picture of an animal that lives at the pond. Cut out your picture.

3 Paste your picture on the painting of a pond. Tell a friend about the animal.

Leveled Activities on back of card
● Below Level
▲ On Level
■ Above Level

More Nonfiction Reading

30 topics aligned with Tennessee Science and Social Studies standards!

MADE FOR TENNESSEE

Setting Up Centers

Science
Center

Materials
nonfiction picture books about fish, mural paper, water colors, Blackline Masters 37–38

Children create a class mural about fish. They can paint the sea background and add a variety of colored fish using Blackline Masters 37–38. See page T93 for this week's Science Center activity.

SC.K.5.2

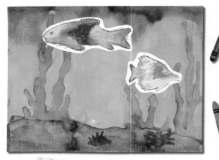

Book
Center

Materials
In the Big Blue Sea

Children work in pairs to compare and contrast the fish pictured in the glossary. Then they look for the different fish in the book and record where the fish appear. See page T99 for this week's Book Center activity.SS4.1.04.b customs and traditions

SC.K.5.2

Writing
Center

Materials
Kinds of Animals chart from Day 1, drawing paper, markers

Children draw pictures of animals listed on the Kinds of Animals chart. Children may also label their pictures with a color word. See page T89 for this week's Writing Center activity.SS4.1.04.b customs and traditions

SC.K.5.2

black bear

Daily Routines

Day at a Glance
T80–T89

Learning to Read

Teacher Read Aloud, *T82*
Phonemic Awareness: /m/, *T86*

Word Work

High-Frequency Word Practice, *T88*

Writing & Oral Language

Oral Language, *T89*

Calendar

Sunday	Monday	Tuesday	Wednesday	Thursday	Friday	Saturday
			1	2	3	4
5	6	7	8	9	10	11
12	13	14	15	16	17	18
19	20	21	22	23	24	25
26	27	28	29	30	31	

Reading the Calendar Discuss today's date. Count the number of Mondays that are in the month. Ask children what they did over the weekend. Have them include any colors they may have seen while they were outside on Saturday and Sunday.

Daily Message

Modeled Writing
As an introduction to today's story, incorporate the colors of children's hats or baseball caps into the daily message.

Joe has a red hat. Erica and Louis have blue caps. Today we will read a story about colored caps.

Word Wall

Ask children to find and read the word they added to the Word Wall last week. Then chant the spelling of the word with children: capital *I* spells *I*, capital *I* spells *I*.

I

A Word Card for this word appears on page R8.

⦿ Daily Phonemic Awareness

Beginning Sounds

- Tell children that they will now play Same Sound Sort. *I will say two words. Listen carefully to find out if the two words begin with the same sound: socks/soup.*
- Remind children that if the words begin with the same sound, they should raise their hands. If the words do not begin with the same sound, they should cover their ears.

Words in Oral Sentences

- Remind children that sentences are made up of words.
- Read this sentence, making a tally mark on the board for each word: *The road is wet.* Have children clap and count the words. Confirm their answers by counting the tally marks on the board.

socks/soup	little/light
moss/pencil	bat/bike
car/puppy	hand/cat
four/find	toad/time

Getting Ready to Learn

To help children plan their day, tell them that they will—

- listen to a story called *Caps of Many Colors.*

- meet a new Alphafriend.

- draw animal pictures in the Writing Center.

OBJECTIVES

- Develop oral language (listening, responding).
- Preview comprehension skill.

Caps of Many Colors

Selection Summary A cap peddler awakens from a nap to find that monkeys in the tree above him have stolen his caps. Furious, the peddler yells, shakes his fists, and stamps his feet, but the monkeys just mimic him. In frustration, he throws his own cap to the ground and, when the monkeys do the same, he retrieves his caps.

Key Concept Playing tricks

This selection presents challenging vocabulary. Before you read, review or introduce a few words: *goods, stack, shade (of color), topple off, balanced, monkeys,* and *fist.*

Teacher Read Aloud

Building Background

Have children tell about monkeys they've seen. Point out that monkeys can do some things humans can because, unlike other animals, they can hold things.

- Display *Caps of Many Colors* and read the title aloud.
- Have children comment on the story art, pointing out the caps and the price tags. Lead children to see that this man sells caps.

COMPREHENSION STRATEGY
Summarize

Teacher Modeling Model the Summarize strategy for children.

Think Aloud When I summarize a story, I tell about the important parts that I have read. As I read, I'll remember the order of what happens. You help me do this, too.

COMPREHENSION SKILL
Inferences: Making Predictions

Teacher Modeling Remind children that good readers think about, or predict, what will happen next in a story. They then check their predictions as they read.

Think Aloud When I look at this picture, I see the man with the caps under a tree. I also see something in the tree over the man's head. Can you guess what is in the tree? Let's read to see if your prediction is correct.

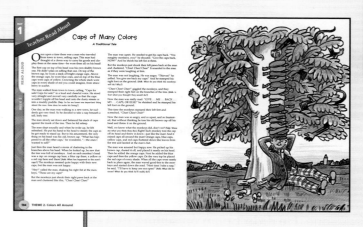

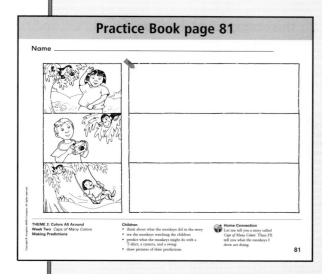

Listening to the Story

Fold your Teacher's Edition so that children can see page T85 as you read. Note that the art is also available on the back of the Theme Poster.

Read the story aloud, emphasizing the actions of the man and the reactions of the monkeys. Pause at the discussion points and allow children to predict what they think will happen next.

Responding

Oral Language: Summarizing the Story Help children summarize parts of the story.

- What happened as the man slept under the tree?
- What did the man do when he saw that the monkeys had taken his caps? What did the monkeys do?
- How did the man get his caps back? Do you think the man planned to do this? Why or why not?
- What was your favorite part of the story?

Practice Book Children will complete **Practice Book** pages 81–82 during small group time.

Practice Book page 81

Practice Book page 82

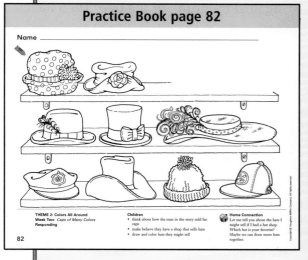

Dramatic Play Center

Materials construction paper

Children can act out *Caps of Many Colors* in the Dramatic Play Center. They can make construction paper caps and use them during their dramatization.

Extra Support/ Intervention

Children who need help summarizing the story may benefit from seeing the illustrations in a picture book retelling of the story, such as *Caps for Sale* by Esphyr Slobodkina.

Teacher Read Aloud **T83**

Caps of Many Colors

A Traditional Tale

Once upon a time there was a man who traveled from town to town, selling caps. This man had thought of a clever way to carry his goods and display them at the same time—he wore them all on his head!

The first cap on top of his head was his own shabby brown one. He didn't plan on selling that one. On top of the brown cap, he wore a stack of bright orange caps. Above the orange caps, he wore blue ones, and on top of the blue caps were caps of yellow. Crowning the whole stack were caps in every shade of red you could imagine, from strawberry to scarlet.

The man walked from town to town, calling, "Caps for sale! Caps for sale!" in a loud and cheerful voice. He stood very straight and moved very carefully so that the caps wouldn't topple off his head and onto the dusty streets or into a muddy puddle. **(Say: So far we know one important thing about the man. How does he make his living?)**

One day, as the man was walking to a new town, he suddenly got very tired. So he decided to take a nap beneath a tall, leafy tree.

The man slowly sat down and balanced his stack of caps against the trunk of the tree. Then he fell asleep.

The man slept soundly and when he woke up, he felt refreshed. He put his hand to his head to steady the caps as he got ready to stand up. But to his amazement, the only thing on his head was his old, brown cap. "What has happened to all the other caps," he wondered, "—the ones I wanted to sell?"

Just then the man heard a storm of chattering in the branches above his head. When he looked up, he saw that the tree was full of monkeys. And on each monkey's head was a cap: an orange cap here, a blue cap there, a yellow or a red cap here and there! **(Ask: What has happened to the man's caps?)** The monkeys seemed quite happy with their new caps, but the man was not happy.

"Hey!" called the man, shaking his right fist at the monkeys, "Those are my caps!"

But the monkeys just shook their right paws back at the man and chattered like this, "Chee! Chee! Chee!"

The man was upset. He needed to get his caps back. "You naughty monkeys, you!" he shouted. "Give the caps back, NOW!" And he shook his left fist at them.

But the monkeys just shook their left paws back at the man and chattered, "Chee! Chee! Chee!" It sounded to the man as if they were laughing at him.

The man was not laughing. He was angry. "Thieves!" he yelled. You give me back my caps!" And he stamped his right foot on the ground. **(Ask: What do you think the monkeys will do? Why?)**

"Chee! Chee! Chee!" giggled the monkeys, and they stamped their right feet on the branches of the tree. **(Ask: Is that what you thought they would do?)**

Now the man was really mad. "GIVE . . . ME . . . BACK . . . MY . . . CAPS, OR ELSE!" he shrieked and he stamped his left foot on the ground.

This time the monkeys stamped their left feet and screeched, "Chee! Chee! Chee!"

Now the man was so angry, and so upset, and so frustrated, that without thinking he tore his old brown cap off his head and threw it on the ground.

Well, we know what the monkeys did, don't we? **(Say: Show me what you think they did.)** Right! Each monkey tore the cap off its head and threw it down—just like the man! And it rained caps all around the man! Orange caps, blue caps, yellow caps, and red caps fluttered down like leaves from the tree and landed at the man's feet.

The man was amazed but happy now. He picked up his brown cap, dusted it off, and placed it neatly on his head. Then he added the orange caps. Next he added the blue caps and then the yellow caps. On the very top he placed the red caps of every shade. When all the caps were neatly back in place again, the man waved good-bye to the monkeys and started down the road. "Next time I take a nap," he said, "I'll have to keep one eye open!" **(Ask: What did he mean? What do you think he'll really do?)**

OBJECTIVES

- Identify pictures whose names begin with /m/.

Materials

- **Alphafriend Cards** *Mimi Mouse, Sammy Seal*
- **Alphafriend CD** Theme 2
- **Alphafolder** *Mimi Mouse*
- **Picture Cards** *man, map, mule, seal, six, sun*
- **Phonics Center** Theme 2, Week 2, Day 1

Alphafolder *Mimi Mouse*

 Home Connection

Hand out the take-home version of Mimi Mouse's Song. Ask children to share the song with their families. (See **Alphafriends Blackline Masters**.)

 English Language Learners

Ask children to name things around the classroom that begin with the /m/ sound. then ask: *Does anyone's name begin with /m/?*

INSTRUCTION

 **PHONEMIC AWARENESS**
Beginning Sound

❶ Teach

Introduce Alphafriend: Mimi Mouse
Use the Alphafriend routine to introduce Mimi Mouse.

▶ **Alphafriend Riddle** Read these clues:

- Our Alphafriend's sound is /m/. Say it with me: /m/.
- This tiny animal has big ears and a small tail.
- She loves to nibble cheese and other snacks.
- She "squeaks" when she sees a cat and runs to hide.

When most hands are up, call on children until they name *mouse*.

▶ **Pocket Chart** Display Mimi Mouse in a pocket chart. Explain that Mimi's sound is /m/. Say her name, stretching the /m/ sound slightly, and have children echo this.

▶ **Alphafriend CD** Play Mimi Mouse's song. Listen for /m/ words.

▶ **Alphafolder** Have children find the /m/ pictures in the scene.

▶ **Summarize**

- What is our Alphafriend's name? What is her sound?
- What words in our Alphafriend's song start with /m/?
- Each time you look at Mimi Mouse this week, remember the /m/ sound.

Mimi Mouse's Song
(tune: This Old Man)

Mimi Mouse, Mimi Mouse, minds her manners in the house.

When she sips her milk, she never makes a mess.

Mud pies never stain her dress.

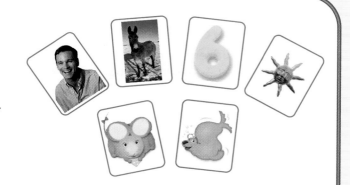

❷ Guided Practice

Listen for /m/ and compare and review /s/.
Display Alphafriend *Sammy Seal* opposite *Mimi Mouse.* Review each character's sound.

Name some pictures.
Children should signal "thumbs up" for each one that begins like Mimi's name. Have children put the card below Mimi's picture. For "thumbs down" words, have children state the beginning sound, /s/, and place the cards below Sammy's picture.

Pictures: *man, map, mule, seal, six, sun*

Tell children that they will sort more pictures in the **Phonics Center** today.

❸ Apply

Have children complete **Practice Book** pages 83–84 at small group time.

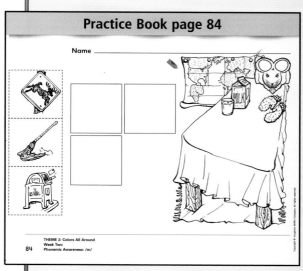

Practice Book page 83

Name _____

THEME 2: Colors All Around
Week Two
Phonemic Awareness: /m/

Children
• fix and color all the pictures on pages 83 and 84 whose names start like *Mimi Mouse*
• cut and paste pictures for that sound in the boxes on page 84
• draw something else whose name starts with that sound

Home Connection
Let's name all the things on the front and back whose names start like *Mimi Mouse.*

83

Practice Book page 84

Name _____

THEME 2: Colors All Around
Week Two
Phonemic Awareness: /m/

84

ABC Phonics Center

Materials Phonics Center materials for Theme 2, Week 2, Day 1 ....

Display Day 1 Direction Chart. Children put *Mimi Mouse* (no letter) in one part of Workmat 2. Then they sort remaining pictures by initial sound: /m/ and not /m/.

- Read high-frequency words.
- Create and write sentences with high-frequency words.

- *Higglety Pigglety: A Book of Rhymes,* page 10
- **Word Card** *I*
- **Picture Cards** *cut, dig, hop, hug, kiss, mix, run, zip*
- **Punctuation Card** period

High-Frequency Word

Display the Word Card for the high-frequency word *I* in a pocket chart.

- Have children read the word and match it on the Word Wall.

- Remind children that the word *I* is often found in books. I'll read a poem. You listen to hear if this word is used in it.

- Read the poem "I Love Colors" on page 10 of *Higglety Pigglety.* Did you hear the word *I* in the poem? Let's see if you can match the Word Card *I* to the word *I* in the poem.

Higglety Pigglety: A Book of Rhymes, page 10

Have children write sentences.

Place the **Word Card** *I* in a pocket chart. Then display the **Picture Cards** *cut, dig, hop, hug, kiss, mix, run,* and *zip.*

- Help children build sentences with the **Word** and **Picture Cards.**

- Children may then write and illustrate one of the sentences or use the cards to create their own sentences with rebus pictures.

ORAL LANGUAGE: VOCABULARY
Using Exact Naming Words

OBJECTIVES
- Use exact nouns.
- Draw and label pictures.

❶ Teach

Discuss naming words.

- Tell children that some words are naming words, or nouns. The word *animal* is a naming word.

- Tell children that some naming words are more exact than others. **Think about the word** *animal.* **When you think about that word, what animals come to mind?**

❷ Practice/Apply

Have children practice using naming words. Write children's responses on a chart titled *Kinds of Animals.*

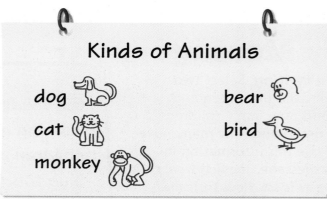

Kinds of Animals

dog

cat

monkey

bear

bird

Writing Center

Materials drawing paper • crayons and markers

Put the chart in the Writing Center. Children can draw and label their own animal pictures. If children want to include color words in their writing, they can refer to the posted color chart.

black bear

Daily Routines

Day at a Glance
T90–T99

Learning to Read

Big Book, *T92*
Phonics: Initial Consonant *m*, *T94*
High Frequency Word: *see, T96*

Word Work

High Frequency Work Practice, *T98*

Writing & Oral Language

Vocabulary Expansion, *T99*

Calendar

Sunday	Monday	Tuesday	Wednesday	Thursday	Friday	Saturday
			1	2	3	4
5	6	7	8	9	10	11
12	13	14	15	16	17	18
19	20	21	22	23	24	25
26	27	28	29	30	31	

Reading the Calendar Write today's date on the board. Ask children to find it on the calendar, and then name yesterday's date and tomorrow's date. Ask several children to tell what plans they have for after school. Model speaking in complete sentences as necessary.

Daily Message

Modeled Writing Select two colors, for example, green and blue. Count how many children have on green and how many have on blue. Use this information in the daily message. **The first word I want to write is** *six*. Since *six* is the first word in my sentence, I will begin it with a capital letter. What letter stands for the sound at the beginning of *six*?

Six children are wearing green. Seven children are wearing blue today.

Word Wall

Have children find and read the word they added to the Word Wall last week. Chant the spelling of the word with children: capital *I* spells *I*.

I

A Word Card for this word appears on page R8.

Daily Phonemic Awareness

Beginning Sounds

- Read "Baa, Baa, Black Sheep" on page 16 of **Higglety Pigglety**. Tell children that they will play a game with beginning sounds. I will say a word from the poem. You listen for the beginning sound and tell me the sound you hear. Now listen: *master.*

- When most hands are up, have children voice the sound. Yes, /m/ is the sound at the beginning of *master.* Continue in a similar manner with other words from the poem: *wool, bags, full, sir, boy, dame, lane.*

Words in Oral Sentences

- Listen: *The van can go fast.* Clap for each word as I say it: *The van can go fast.* How many words did you hear? Yes, five words.

- Repeat with these sentences: *I like my new gray cat; The big vase is blue.*

Baa, Baa, Black Sheep
Baa, baa, black sheep,
Have you any wool?
Yes, sir, yes, sir,
Three bags full,
One for the master,
One for the dame,
One for the little boy
Who lives in the lane.
a Mother Goose Rhyme
16

Higglety Pigglety: A Book of Rhymes, page 16

Getting Ready to Learn

To help children plan their day, tell them that they will—

- listen to a **Big Book:** *In the Big Blue Sea.*

- learn the new letters *M* and *m,* and see words that begin with *m.*

- explore fish in the Science Center.

OBJECTIVES

- Introduce concepts of print.
- Develop story language.
- Reinforce comprehension strategy and comprehension skill.

Big Book

In the Big Blue Sea

by Chyng Feng Sun
Photography by Norbert Wu

Includes:
Science Link

Big Blue Sea

Selection Summary In this photo essay, children are invited to accompany Norbert Wu as he photographs colorful fish in the ocean.

Key Concept Shapes, sizes, and colors of fish

English Language Learners

Discuss the meaning of *dive* and *swim* by asking children to mime the actions. Review colors by playing a matching game using pictures of differently colored fish and color word cards.

INSTRUCTION

Reading the Big Book

Building Background

Ask children to tell what they know about fish. Encourage them to include observations made from watching fish in a fish tank, at an aquarium, or in a lake, pond, or ocean. Then introduce the book *In the Big Blue Sea*.

COMPREHENSION STRATEGY
Summarize

Teacher Modeling Remind children that good readers remember important story parts to retell a story and help them understand it better. Model the Summarize strategy.

Think Aloud I can tell from the title and from the picture that this book tells about real things found in the ocean. When I read a book about real things, I pay attention to information I can retell or share after reading. As I read, you think about this, too.

COMPREHENSION SKILL
Inferences: Making Predictions

Teacher Modeling Review that good readers predict what a book will be about before they read.

Think Aloud I wonder what *In the Big Blue Sea* is about. The title mentions the big blue sea and the picture shows real fish. I think the story tells about real things in the sea. As I look at the first few pictures, I think that I may be right. The pictures show real people and more fish.

Big Book Read Aloud

Read the selection aloud, tracking the print as you read. Pause for children to study the beautiful photographs and comment on the fish.

Responding

Oral Language: Personal Response Encourage children to use the language of the story as they react to it.

- How are the fish in the story alike? How are they different?
- Which fish is your favorite? Why?

Science Center

Materials nonfiction picture books about fish • mural paper • water colors • Blackline Masters 37–38 • crayons ....

Have children create a class mural about fish. Children can paint the background with water colors. Then, using **Blackline Masters 37–38** as a guide, have them color or paint fish to add to the mural. Some children may want to refer to *In the Big Blue Sea* or other picture books to help them draw or label specific fish.

Extra Support/ Intervention

Some children may not be familiar with the special equipment used to snorkel or dive underwater. Preview the pictures to identify the equipment and explain its use.

OBJECTIVES

- Identify words that begin with /m/.
- Identify pictures whose names start with the letter *m*.
- Form the letters *M, m*.

Materials

- **Alphafriend Card** *Mimi Mouse*
- **Letter Cards** *m, s*
- **Picture Cards** *man, map, mop, sandbox, sandwich, six, sun*
- **Blackline Master** 169
- **Phonics Center** Theme 2, Week 2, Day 2

Mimi Mouse's Song
(tune: This Old Man)

Mimi Mouse, Mimi Mouse, minds
her manners in the house.

When she sips her milk, she
never makes a mess.

Mud pies never stain her dress.

**Extra Support/
Intervention**

To help children remember the sound for
m, point out that the letter's name gives
a clue to its sound: *m*, /m/.

TARGET SKILL PHONICS
Initial Consonant *m*

❶ Phonemic Awareness Warm-Up

Beginning Sound Read or sing the lyrics to Mimi Mouse's song
and have children echo it line-for-line. Have them listen for the
/m/ words and point to their mouths each time they hear one. See
Theme Resources page R3 for music and lyrics.

❷ Teach Phonics

Beginning Letter Display the Mimi Mouse card,
and have children name the letter on the picture.
The letter *m* stands for the sound /m/, as in *mouse*.
When you see an *m*, remember Mimi Mouse. That
will help you remember the sound /m/.

Write *mouse* on the board, underlining the *m*.
What is the first letter in the word *mouse*? *Mouse*
starts with /m/, so *m* is the first letter I write for *mouse*.

❸ Guided Practice

Compare and review: *s* In a pocket chart, display the *Mimi
Mouse* card with **Letter Card** *m* beside it. Place the **Letter Card** *s*
next to the *m*. Place the **Picture Cards** in random order. Children
can name a picture, say the beginning sound and letter, and then
put the card either below the *m* or the *s*. Tell children they will sort
more pictures in the **Phonics Center** today.

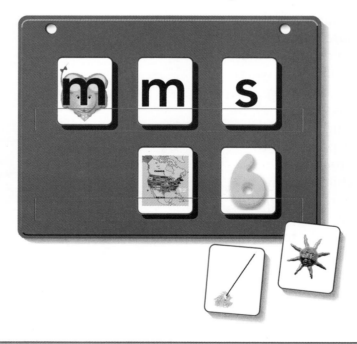

Penmanship Rhyme: M

Make a line going down.
Then two lines that meet.
One more, you're done.
It's very neat.

Penmanship Rhyme: m

Little *m* is short.
Start in the middle.
Make two little hills.
It's not a riddle.

Penmanship: Writing M, m Tell children that now they'll learn to write the letters that stand for /m/: capital *M* and small *m*. Write each letter as you recite the penmanship rhyme. Children can chant each rhyme as they "write" the letter in the air.

❹ Apply

Have children complete **Practice Book** page 85 at small group time. For additional penmanship practice assign **Blackline Master** 169. Penmanship practice for the continuous stroke style is available on **Blackline Master** 195.

Practice Book page 85

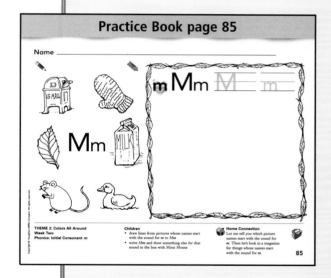

ABC Phonics Center

Materials Phonics Center materials for Theme 2, Week 2, Day 2 ....

Display Day 2 Direction Chart. Children put *Mimi Mouse* (with letter) in one part of Workmat 2. Then they sort remaining pictures by initial letter: *m* and not *m*.

HIGH-FREQUENCY WORD
New Word: *see*

OBJECTIVES
• Read and write the high-frequency word *see*.

Materials
• **Word Cards** *I, see*
• **Picture Cards** *berries, jam, toast*
• **Punctuation Card** period
• *Higglety Pigglety: A Book of Rhymes,* pages 44–45

❶ Teach

Introduce the word *see*. Tell children that today they will learn to read and write the word *see*, a word often used in stories. Say *see* and use it in context.

> I *see* our classroom.   I can *see* you.   Can you *see* me?

• Write *see* on the board, and have children spell it as you point to each letter. Spell *see* with me, *s-e-e.* Then lead children in a chant, clapping on each beat, to help them remember how *see* is spelled: *s-e-e, see! s-e-e, see.*

Word Wall Ask children to help you decide where on the Word Wall *see* should be posted. As needed, prompt children by pointing out that *see* begins with the letter *s*. Add *see* to the Word Wall. Remind children to look there when they need to remember how to write the word.

❷ Guided Practice

Build these sentences one at a time. Build the following sentences in a pocket chart. Have children take turns reading the sentences aloud. Leave the pocket chart out so that children can practice building and reading sentences.

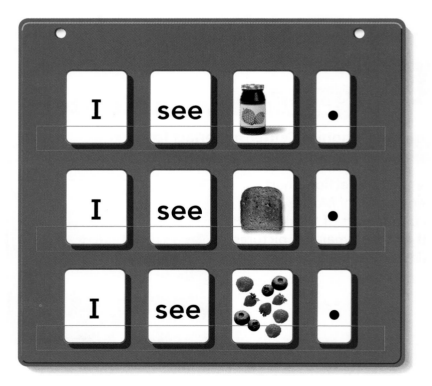

Display *Higglety Pigglety: A Book of Rhymes*, pages 44–45.

- Share the poem "Rhyme" aloud.

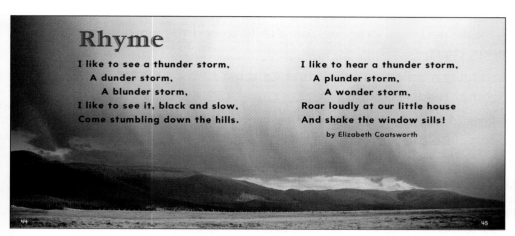

Rhyme

I like to see a thunder storm,
  A dunder storm,
   A blunder storm,
I like to see it, black and slow,
Come stumbling down the hills.

I like to hear a thunder storm,
  A plunder storm,
   A wonder storm,
Roar loudly at our little house
And shake the window sills!

by Elizabeth Coatsworth

Higglety Pigglety: A Book of Rhymes, pages 44–45

- Reread the poem, asking children to listen for the word *see*. **I'll read the poem one more time. This time, listen for the word *see*. If you hear the word *see*, raise your hand.**

- Call on children to point to the word *see* each time it appears in the poem.

❸ Apply

- Have children complete **Practice Book** page 86 at small group time.

- Pass out copies of **Practice Book** pages 195–196, *I See*. Read the title aloud. Ask children where this story takes place.

- For each page, have children look at the picture and tell what the characters are doing. Have them read the page silently. Then ask a child to read the page aloud. Use questions such as the following to prompt discussion:

  Pages 1–4 What are the characters using to make their pictures? What do you like to use to make a picture?

- Then have children count the number of times the word *see* is used in the story.

Practice Book page 86

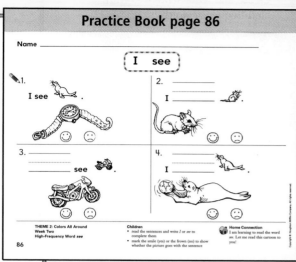

Practice Book pages 195–196

Monitoring Student Progress

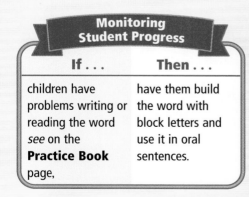

If . . .	Then . . .
children have problems writing or reading the word *see* on the **Practice Book** page,	have them build the word with block letters and use it in oral sentences.

OBJECTIVES

- Read high-frequency words.
- Create and write sentences with high-frequency words.

Materials

- **Word Cards** *I, see*
- **Picture Cards** color words; *berries, ink, jam, sandals, toast, toys, watermelon*
- **Punctuation Card** *period*

PRACTICE

High-Frequency Words

Tell children that you want them to help build sentences.

- Display the **Picture Cards** and **Word Cards** in random order at the bottom of a pocket chart. Review the words together.

- I want the first word in the sentence to be *I*. Who can find that word?

- I want the next word to be *see.* Ask a child to add the word *see* to the pocket chart.

- Then have a child add the **Picture Card** *red* to the pocket chart. Together read: *I see red _____ .*

- How could we finish the sentence? Invite a child to select a **Picture Card** to complete the sentence.

- Read the sentence together, and then continue building other sentences.

Have children write sentences.

- Have children copy the sentence stem and choose a color word.

- Have children complete the sentence by drawing a picture of something that is that color. Some children may refer to the Color Chart to write the color word.

VOCABULARY EXPANSION
Using Exact Naming Words

Listening/Speaking/Viewing

Discuss exact naming words.

- Ask children to recall the **Big Book** *In the Big Blue Sea*. Point out that the word *fish* is a naming word. Page through the book and have children describe some of the fish. Remind them to speak in complete sentences.

- Remind children that some nouns are more exact than others. Display pages 18–19 of *In the Big Blue Sea* and read the names of the fish for children.

- Tell children that these words more clearly name the fish in the book.

- Allow children time to match a few of the fish on pages 18–19 to the fish in the selection. Ask, for example: Which words more clearly name the fish on page 4, *green fish* or *queen angelfish*?

OBJECTIVES
- Use exact words for fish.

Materials
- **Big Book** *In the Big Blue Sea*

Vocabulary Support

The Vocabulary Reader can be used to develop and reinforce vocabulary related to the instruction for this week.

Book Center

Materials *In the Big Blue Sea*

Pairs of children can compare other fish in the glossary to those in the big book. One child can point to a specific fish, and the child's partner can locate it in the book. Together they can make a list of the fish they locate.

DAY **2**

VOCABULARY   WEEK 2

Day at a Glance
T100–T113

Learning to Read

Big Book, *T102*
Phonics: Initial Consonant *m*, *T108*

Word Work

Exploring Words, *T112*

Writing & Oral Language

Shared Writing, *T113*

Daily Routines

Sunday	Monday	Tuesday	Wednesday	Thursday	Friday	Saturday
			1	2	3	4
5	6	7	8	9	10	11
12	13	14	15	16	17	18
19	20	21	22	23	24	25
26	27	28	29	30	31	

Calendar

Reading the Calendar After completing the calendar routine, explore the colors in the classroom. What green things can you see in the classroom? Is anyone wearing a green shirt? Is it a light or dark shade of green?

Daily Message

Modeled Writing Talk about the color of the day. Use some of your morning discussion in the message. Call on children to name known letters. See the sample message.

Good morning!
Paul made us a
green snack.
Rikki brought
green juice.

Word Wall

Ask children if they can find the new word they added to the Word Wall yesterday. Call on a child to point it out. Have children chant the spelling of the word: *s-e-e* spells *see.* Then have children find and spell *I*: capital *I* spells *I*.

I		see

Word Cards for these words appear on page R8.

🎯 Daily Phonemic Awareness

Beginning Sounds

- Let's listen for beginning sounds. I will say two words, and you tell me which word begins with Mimi Mouse's sound, /m/. Listen: *marble, jack*.

- Say the words with me: *marble, jack*. Which word begins with /m/? . . . Yes, *marble* begins with /m/.

- Continue with the words shown.

Words in Oral Sentences

- Read aloud "Hickory Dickory Dock," page 24 of **Higglety Pigglety: A Book of Rhymes**.

- Tell me how many words I say. Clap the words. *The mouse ran up the clock.* Repeat with *The clock struck one.*

map/girl	cook/meat
middle/top	sand/mine
mat/fork	good/mean
car/man	move/sweet

Getting Ready to Learn

To help children plan their day, tell them that they will—

- reread and talk about the **Big Book:** *In the Big Blue Sea.*

- tell a story called "Look at Me!"

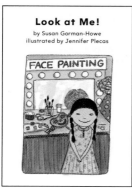

Look at Me!
by Susan Gorman-Howe
illustrated by Jennifer Plecas

- make a fish mobile in the Art Center

Reading the Big Book

Reading for Understanding

Reread the story, emphasizing the rhyme, rhythm, and the color words. Point out words like *splish* and *splash* that sound like the sounds they stand for. Pause for discussion points.

I will swim in the big blue sea!
Come along and swim with me.

1

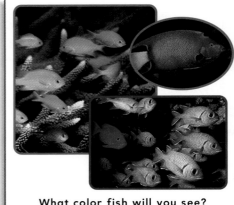

What color fish will you see?

What color fish would you like to be?

2

3

Dive and swim,
splish, *splash*, splish!
Would you be a green fish?

Dive and swim,
splish, *splash*, splish!
Would you be a red fish?

4

5

Extra Support/Intervention

If children have trouble naming the colors in the fish, have them practice matching color swatches and naming the colors with a partner.

Dive and swim,
splish, *splash*, splish!
Would you be a yellow fish?

6

Dive and swim,
splish, *splash*, splish!
Would you be an orange fish?

7

What color fish will you see?

8

What color fish would you like to be?

9

Dive and swim,
splish, *splash*, splish!
Would you be a white fish?

10

Dive and swim,
splish, *splash*, splish!
Would you be a blue fish?

11

CRITICAL THINKING
Guiding Comprehension

page 1

- **NOTING DETAILS** The man on this page is Norbert Wu. He took the pictures for this story. What things does Norbert Wu use to take his underwater pictures?

TARGET SKILL

COMPREHENSION SKILL
Inferences: Making Predictions

pages 2–3

Teacher-Student Modeling Read aloud the text on pages 2–3. Have children use the questions to predict what fish they will read about on the following pages. *What color fish will you see?*

TARGET SKILL

COMPREHENSION STRATEGY
Summarize

pages 4–7
Teacher-Student Modeling Remind children that good readers think about the important information in a story to help them remember the story and tell about it later. Prompts: *What kind of fish have we read about so far?* (green, red, yellow, orange)

CRITICAL THINKING
Guiding Comprehension

pages 8–9

- **COMPARE AND CONTRAST** How are the fish on these pages alike? How are they different?

COMPREHENSION STRATEGY

Summarize

pages 16–17

Student Modeling What does Norbert Wu do? What are some of the fish he took pictures of?

REVISITING THE TEXT

Concepts of Print

pages 14–16

Capitalize First Word in Sentence; End Punctuation

- Read the sentence on page 14. Frame *What*. Why does *What* begin with a capital letter?

- What kind of sentence is this? How do you know? (asking sentence; asks question, ends with a question mark)

- Repeat with the sentence on page 16. Have children note the use of a capital letter to begin the sentence and identify the end mark as a period.

Dive and swim, splish, *splash*, splish! Would you be a purple fish? 12

Dive and swim, splish, *splash*, splish! Would you be a black fish? 13

12   **13**

What color fish did you see? 14

What color fish would you like to be? 15

14   **15**

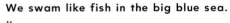

We swam like fish in the big blue sea. 16

I'm so glad you swam with me! 17

16   **17**

NAME: **Queen Angelfish**
HABITAT: Caribbean

NAME: **Blue Spotted Grouper**
HABITAT: Indo-Pacific

NAME: **Redback Butterflyfish**
HABITAT: Red Sea

NAME: **Powder Blue Surgeonfish**
HABITAT: Indo-Pacific

NAME: **Three-spotted Angelfish**
HABITAT: Indo-Pacific

NAME: **Clownfish**
HABITAT: Indo-Malaysian Archipelago to Japan

NAME: **Blackcap Basslet**
HABITAT: Bahamas, northwestern and southern Caribbean

NAME: **Juvenile French Angelfish**
HABITAT: Caribbean

18

19

CRITICAL THINKING
Guiding Comprehension

pages 18–19

- **COMPARE AND CONTRAST** Discuss with children how these pages are different from the other pages in the selection. Explain that books that tell about real things sometimes have a special book part called a *glossary*. The glossary tells more about the things in the book.

 **COMPREHENSION SKILL**

Inferences: Making Predictions

pages 2–19

Student Modeling Have children browse through the book and point out places where they were able to predict what they would see or read about next. Ask children to tell what clues they used to make their predictions.

 English Language Learners

Distribute the color **Picture Cards** to partners. Have partners browse through the book and match the cards to the colors in the story.

Practice Book page 87

Responding

Oral Language: Retelling

Use these prompts to help children retell the selection:

- What did Norbert Wu do at the beginning of the book?

- What fish did Norbert Wu and the children see?

- How do color words help you to remember the kinds of fish you saw?

Practice Book Children will complete **Practice Book** page 87 page at small group time.

Oral Language: Literature Circle Have small groups discuss what might happen if the book were to continue. What other fish might Norbert Wu see? What color would these fish be?

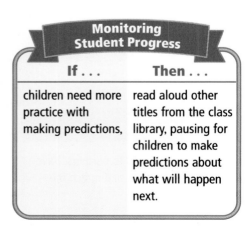

Monitoring Student Progress

If . . .	Then . . .
children need more practice with making predictions,	read aloud other titles from the class library, pausing for children to make predictions about what will happen next.

Art Center

Materials Blackline Masters 37–38 • paints and brushes • crayons or markers • string • coat hangers • *In the Big Blue Sea* ....

Use **Blackline Masters 37–38** to prepare fish shapes that resemble the fish in *In the Big Blue Sea*. Display pages 18–19 of the **Big Book** in the Art Center. Ask children to match the fish shapes to the fish on the glossary page and paint the fish accordingly. Then hang the fish from varying lengths of string tied to the hangers to create fish mobiles.

OBJECTIVES

- Identify words that begin with /m/.
- Identify pictures whose names start with the letter *m*.

Materials

- **Alphafriend Card** *Mimi Mouse*
- **Alphafriend CD** Theme 2
- **Picture Cards** for *m* and assorted others

Mimi Mouse's Song

(tune: This Old Man)

Mimi Mouse, Mimi Mouse, minds
her manners in the house.

When she sips her milk, she
never makes a mess.

Mud pies never stain her dress.

Extra Support/ Intervention

Read "I Went Upstairs," on page 12 of *Higglety Pigglety*. Have children touch a finger to their mouths each time they hear a word that begins with /m/. Then call on children to point to words that begin with *m* in the rhyme.

PHONICS
Initial Consonant *m*

❶ Phonemic Awareness Warm-Up

Beginning Sound Read the lyrics to Mimi Mouse's song aloud, and have children echo it line-for-line. Have them listen for the /m/ words.

- Tell children that you will read the song again slowly. This time, if you hear a word that begins with /m/ raise your hand. If you hear another /m/ word, put your hand down. We'll do this each time we hear an /m/ word.

- As needed, model raising and lowering your hand alternately for /m/ words as you read the first line. Then reread the song, having children raise and lower their hands for /m/ words.

❷ Teach Phonics

Beginning Letter *m* Display the *Mimi Mouse* card and have children name the letter on the picture.

- What letter stands for the sound /m/, as in *mouse*? Who can help you remember the sound /m/?

- Write *mouse* on the board, underlining the *m*. What is the first letter in the word *mouse*? (m) *Mouse* starts with /m/, so *m* is the first letter I write for *mouse*.

❸ Guided Practice/Apply

- Write *Mm* on the board and circle it. Then write *Mm*, circle it, and draw a line through it to show "not *m*."

- Distribute **Picture Cards** for *m* and assorted others, one to a child, to a small group of children.

- In turn, children name their picture, say the beginning sound, and stand below the correct symbol on the board. Children without **Picture Cards** verify their decisions.

- Repeat the activity with different groups of children until each child has a chance to name a picture, say the beginning sound, and stand below the correct symbol on the board.

HOUGHTON MIFFLIN
Reading

Wordless Book

Phonics Library

Colors All Around

Look at Me!

by Susan Gorman-Howe
illustrated by Jennifer Plecas

FACE PAINTING

9

PHONICS LIBRARY
Storytelling Practice

Building Background

Let's look at the title page. The title is "Look at Me!" I see brushes and paints in the picture. What do you think they will be used for? Help children identify the face painting tools, such as the brushes, water, and face powder. Ask children what things they see on the title page whose names begin with /m/. (mirror, makeup, mask)

Preview the pictures on pages 10–11. Have children look to see a few of the characters and to predict what the story is about.

OBJECTIVES

- Tell a wordless story.
- Find pictures whose names begin with /m/.

10

11

Oral Language

Go back to page 9. Then page through the story and have children help tell what's happening as they carefully view each picture. Use prompts such as these to help children tell the story:

page 10 This girl is having her face painted. What colors has the painter used? (red and white)

page 11 What is the green shape on this boy's face? (a star)

page 12 The painter is painting whiskers on the boy's face. Does he remind you of any animal you know?

page 13 Do you think the children like how they look? How can you tell? (Yes, because they are smiling at themselves in the mirror.)

pages 14–15 Who is the face painter? What do you think the children are going to do now? (The face painter is a clown. The children will be in a circus.)

Now have children take turns retelling the story page by page.

Phonics Connection

Now let's go back and look at each page. Raise your hand when you see something whose name begins with Mimi Mouse's sound, /m-m-m/. (makeup, mirror, mouth)

Home Connection

Children can color the pictures whose names begin with the /m/ in the take-home version of "Look at Me!" After retelling on Day 4, they can take it home to share with family members. (See **Phonics Library Blackline Masters**.)

12

13

14

15

Storytelling Practice T111

OBJECTIVES

• Explore color words.

Materials

• **Read Aloud** *Caps of Many Colors*

INSTRUCTION

EXPLORING WORDS
Color Words

Discuss shades of colors.

• Ask children to look at the picture of the man with his caps as you read *Caps of Many Colors*. Then reread the second paragraph, which describes the color of the caps, aloud.

• Reread the last sentence of the paragraph: *Crowning the whole stack were caps in every shade of red you could imagine, from strawberry to scarlet.*

• Begin a discussion of shades of color with children. Use words like *bright, light,* and *dark.* Define *strawberry red* as a deep, dark red and *scarlet* as a bright, fiery red.

• Repeat the expression *strawberry red.* Mention to children that when people want you to have a clear idea of a color they are talking about, they may compare it to something else. Ask children if they have ever heard of colors like *sky blue, lemon yellow,* and *lime green.*

Brainstorm shades of colors.

• Point to various items in the classroom and ask children to describe the color of the item by comparing it to something else. List their suggestions on chart paper, organizing the phrases by color.

• Have children choose one of the color phrases from the chart to illustrate. Allow time for children to share and describe their drawings to the class.

SHARED WRITING
Writing a Description

OBJECTIVES
- Use color words to describe fish mobiles.

Materials
- **Big Book** *In the Big Blue Sea*

Use fish mobiles to describe colors and patterns.

- Display the fish mobiles children made in the Art Center today. Tell children that they are going to describe the different types of fish that they see.

- Remind children to look for patterns or shades of color on the fish to help them with their descriptions.

- Begin by pointing to a fish and describing it. I see a fire-engine red fish. What do you see? Then hand a small beanbag to a child to show that it is his or her turn. As children describe the fish, record their answers on chart paper.

- If needed, prompt children to complete their descriptions. Is the fish a bright color? a pale color? Does the fish have spots?

I see a _____ fish.
What do you see?

fire engine red

grape purple

sunny yellow

Day at a Glance
T114–T121

Learning to Read

Big Book, *T116*

Phonics: Review Initial
Consonant *m, T118*

Word Work

Exploring Words, *T120*

Writing &
Oral Language

Interactive Writing, *T121*

Daily Routines

Sunday	Monday	Tuesday	Wednesday	Thursday	Friday	Saturday
			1	2	3	4
5	6	7	8	9	10	11
12	13	14	15	16	17	18
19	20	21	22	23	24	25
26	27	28	29	30	31	

Calendar

Reading the Calendar Have an individual find today's date on the calendar. Then ask questions about the month. How many days have there been since the first day of the month? How many days are there until the end of the month?

Daily Message

Modeled Writing
Use some words that begin with *m* in today's message. Have children circle the *m*'s they see.

This morning we will measure ourselves in the Math Center.

Word Wall

Ask children to find and read the words that they've added to the Word Wall. Ask them to tell why the words are placed where they are.

I	see

Word Cards for these words appear on page R8.

Daily Phonemic Awareness

Beginning Sounds

- Listen as I say two words: *money, milk*. Say the words with me: *money, milk*. Do you hear the same sound at the beginning of both words? . . . Yes, *money* and *milk* begin with the same sound. Help children isolate the beginning sound, /m/.

- Now play What's the Sound? Say the two words in each pair shown. For each pair, have children isolate and identify the beginning sound.

tiger/turkey	raisin/red
mittens/muffins	table/telephone
banana/boy	pencil/penny
balloon/butter	

Words in Oral Sentences

- You know that words are made of sounds. What are sentences made of? (words) Pat your knees for each word you hear in this sentence: *A hen lays eggs*. How many words did you hear? (four)

- Let's try another one. Be careful. This one has a word with two parts in it. Pat just once for the whole word. *The pig has five piglets*. Good! There are six sounds but only five words. Continue with other simple sentences.

Getting Ready to Learn

To help children plan their day, tell them that they will—

- read the Science Link: *What Do You Do, Norbert Wu?*

- sort *m* words in the **Phonics Center**.

- retell a book called "Look at Me!"

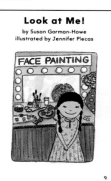

OBJECTIVES

- Make predictions.
- Recognize use of capital letter at the beginning of a sentence.
- Recognize use of end punctuation: period, question mark.

Big Book

What Do You Do, Norbert Wu?

Science Link

Reading

In the Big Blue Sea

by Chyng Feng Sun
Photography by Norbert Wu

Includes Science Link

Oral Language

click The sound a camera makes when you push the button to take a picture. *Click* is a word that stands for the sound it makes.

English Language Learners

Discuss photography with children. Say the word and have children say it with you. Mention that when people take photographs they usually say *take pictures.* You may also wish to introduce underwater vocabulary.

READING THE BIG BOOK
Science Link

Building Background

Ask children to tell if they know the word that names someone who takes pictures. Then have them talk about photographs they have seen or have taken.

- Read aloud the title and discuss the cover.
- Recall that Norbert Wu took the photographs for *In the Big Blue Sea.* Which picture shows Norbert Wu underwater? Which picture shows him out of the water?

Reading for Understanding Pause for discussion as you share the selection.

 COMPREHENSION STRATEGY
Summarize

Student Modeling Remind children that they have to listen for important information in order to summarize or tell about a selection. Ask: What will you look for as we read the selection?

 COMPREHENSION SKILL
Inferences: Making Predictions

Student Modeling Remind children that good readers make predictions about a story and check their predictions as they read. Ask: How can the pictures on the title page help you predict what Norbert Wu does? How can you check your predictions?

I am a photographer.
I take pictures.

22

I see a shark!
Click!

23

I see a starfish!
Click!

24

I see seals!
Click!

25

I took these pictures of fish.
Can you find them in this book?

26

CRITICAL THINKING

Guiding Comprehension

pages 22–23

- **NOTING DETAILS** What does a photographer do? What kind of photographer is Norbert Wu?

pages 24–25

- **INFERENCES: DRAWING CONCLUSIONS** Why do you think Norbert Wu takes pictures of starfish and seals?

page 26

- **COMPARE AND CONTRAST** How are these fish the same? different?

TARGET SKILL

REVISITING THE TEXT

Concepts of Print

page 28

Capitalize First Word in Sentence; End Punctuation

- Frame and read *I took these pictures of fish.* **What kind of sentence is this? How can you tell?** (telling sentence; It ends with a period.)

- Frame and read *Can you find them in this book?* **Why does the word** *Can* **begin with a capital letter?** (It is the first word in the sentence.) **What kind of sentence is this? How can you tell?** (asking sentence; question mark)

Responding

Oral Language: Summarizing Have children respond to the title question as they summarize the selection.

OBJECTIVES

- Identify words that begin with /m/.

Materials

- *From Apples to Zebras: A Book of ABC's,* page 14
- **Alphafriend Card** *Mimi Mouse, Sammy Seal*
- **Alphafolder** *Mimi Mouse*
- **Letter Card** *m, s*
- **Picture Cards** *man, map, mule, salt, seal, six, sun*
- **Phonics Center** Theme 2, Week 2, Day 4

PRACTICE

PHONICS
Review Initial Consonant *m*

Phonemic Awareness: Review Beginning Sound Display the scene in Mimi Mouse's Alphafolder. One thing I see in Mimi's kitchen is a mug. Say *mug* with me. Does *mug* begin with the same sound as Mimi Mouse, /m/? Call on children to point to and name other items in the picture that begin with /m/.

From Apples to Zebras: A Book of ABC's, **page 14**

Review consonant *m* Using self-stick notes, cover the words on page 14 of *From Apples to Zebras: A Book of ABC's.* Then display the page.

- Ask children what letter they expect to see at the beginning of each word and why.
- Uncover the words so that children can check their predictions.

Home Connection

Challenge children to look at home for items or for names that begin with the consonant *m*. Children can draw pictures to show what they have found.

Practice/Apply In a pocket chart, display the cards for *Mimi Mouse* and *Sammy Seal* and the **Letter Cards** *m* and *s*.

- Review the sound for *m, /m/* and *s, /s/.*

- Hold up **Picture Cards** one at a time. Have children name a picture, say the beginning sound, and place the card below the correct letter.

Pictures: *seal, map, six, mule, salt, mix, sun, man*

- Tell children they will sort more pictures in the **Phonics Center** today.

- Have children complete **Practice Book** page 88 at small group time.

- In groups today, children will also identify pictures whose names begin with /m/ as they retell the **Phonics Library** story "Look at Me!" See suggestions, pages T109–T111.

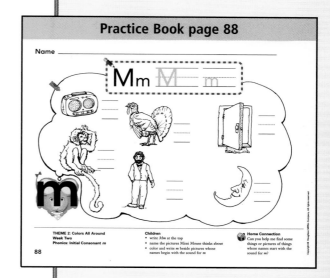

Practice Book page 88

Name _____

M m M m

THEME 2: Colors All Around
Week Two
Phonics: Initial Consonant *m*

Children
• write *Mm* at the top
• name the pictures Mimi Mouse thinks about
• color and write *m* beside pictures whose names begin with the sound for *m*

Home Connection
Can you help me find some things or pictures of things whose names start with the sound for *m*?

88

ABC Phonics Center

Materials Phonics Center materials for Theme 2, Week 2, Day 4 ·

Display Day 4 Direction Chart. Children put **Letter Cards** *m* and *s* in separate sections of Workmat 2. Then they sort remaining pictures by initial letter: *m* and *s*.

Monitoring Student Progress

If . . .	Then . . .
children have trouble identifying /m/ words,	have them work with you or a partner to name items in the **Alphafolder** scene.

OBJECTIVES

- Explore color words.

EXPLORING WORDS
Color Words

Make a chart of color words together.

- Display the chart children used during yesterday's Exploring Words activity. (See page T112.) Read through the chart with children.

- Recall with children that in *Caps of Many Colors,* the peddler had caps in many shades of red, from strawberry to scarlet. Explain to children that some color words, like *strawberry red,* use common things to help describe how light, dark, or bright they are. Other color words, like *scarlet,* are special color words used to name a shade of color.

- Brainstorm other color words with children. You may want to read the color words on some crayons.

- Add any new color words to the chart.

red	orange	yellow	green	blue	purple	pink

red	orange	yellow	green	blue	purple	pink
scarlet	sunset	lemon	kelly	aqua	violet	fuchsia
burgundy ruby	tangerine	gold	emerald	turquoise denim	mauve maroon	magenta

Have children draw pictures of themselves wearing favorite clothes. Allow time for children to share and describe their drawings. Encourage children to choose color words that will help people know just what shade of color they are talking about.

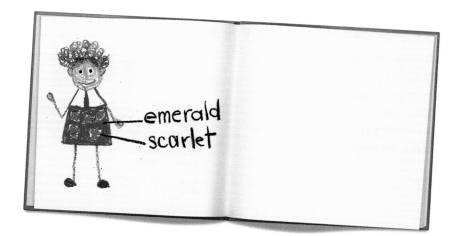

INTERACTIVE WRITING
Writing a Description

Prepare to write a description together.

- Display and read the chart from yesterday's Shared Writing activity. (See page T113.)

- Work with children to write a story about the colorful fish listed on the chart, or the fish Norbert Wu photographed for his book.

- As you write, ask children to write the beginning consonants *s* and *m*. They can also add the appropriate end punctuation.

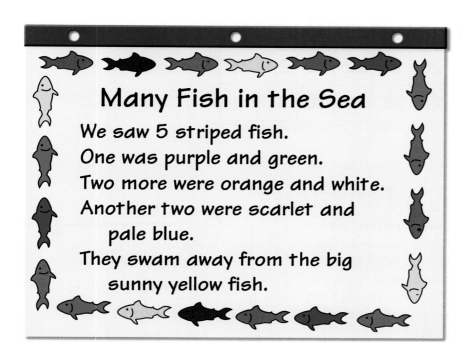

Many Fish in the Sea

We saw 5 striped fish.
One was purple and green.
Two more were orange and white.
Another two were scarlet and
    pale blue.
They swam away from the big
    sunny yellow fish.

Day at a Glance
T122–T129

Learning to Read

Revisiting the Literature, *T124*
Phonics Review: Initial Consonants *m, s, T126*

Word Work

Exploring Words, *T128*

Writing & Oral Language

Independent Writing, *T129*

Daily Routines

Sunday	Monday	Tuesday	Wednesday	Thursday	Friday	Saturday
			1	**2**	**3**	**4**
5	**6**	**7**	**8**	**9**	**10**	**11**
12	**13**	**14**	**15**	**16**	**17**	**18**
19	**20**	**21**	**22**	**23**	**24**	**25**
26	**27**	**28**	**29**	**30**	**31**	

Calendar

Reading the Calendar As children share the colored items they've worn today, encourage them to use color words that more clearly define the shade of their clothing.

Daily Message

Interactive Writing Have children help you write the daily message. What kind of letter should I use to begin my sentence? . . . How should I end each sentence, with a period or a question mark?

Ms. Sullivan's favorite color is blue. What is your favorite color?

Our Favorite Colors

| Ms. Sullivan | blue |
| Tommy | green |

Word Wall

Read the Word Wall together, and then play a rhyming game: Find a word that rhymes with *my* . . . Yes, *I* rhymes with *my*. Find a word that rhymes with *tree* . . . Yes, *see* rhymes with *tree*.

| I | see |

Word Cards for these words appear on page R8.

Daily Phonemic Awareness

Beginning Sounds

- Play Same Sound Sort with children. I will say two words. Listen carefully to find out if the two words begin with the same sound.

- If the words begin with the same sound, raise your hands. If the words do not begin with the same sound, cover your ears. Using the words shown here, ask children to say the beginning sounds.

Words in Oral Sentences

- Tell children you'll say a silly sentence. They will clap their hands for each word. Have children count the claps and whisper the answer to a partner. Use these silly sentences:

A big fat dog said "Boo!"   *A cow ate my book.*

mix/beat	car/man
robot/rain	fish/feather
rain/room	hand/hammer
bugs/beach	boxes/carts
men/mops	boat/book

Getting Ready to Learn

To help children plan their day, tell them that they will—

- reread and talk about all the books they've read this week.

- take home a story they can retell.

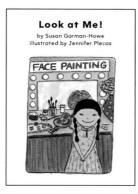

Look at Me!
by Susan Gorman-Howe
illustrated by Jennifer Plecas

FACE PAINTING

- write about a career choice in their journals.

Sam's Journal

OBJECTIVES

● Review the week's selections.

REVISITING THE LITERATURE
Literature Discussion

Review the week's selections, using these suggestions.

● Have children retell *Caps of Many Colors* in their own words. Ask how the man was able to get his caps back from the monkeys.

● Display *In the Big Blue Sea*. Have children describe the fish in the book.

● Call on children to answer the question *What Do You Do, Norbert Wu?* Allow children to tell if they would like a job like Norbert Wu's.

● Together, retell the story "Look at Me!" Ask children to name the /m/ pictures in the story.

● Ask children to vote for their favorite book of the week. Then read the text of the winner aloud.

COMPREHENSION SKILL
Making Predictions

Compare Books Remind children that good readers predict what a book is about before reading and predict what will happen next while reading. Browse through each story, asking how children were able to make predictions. For example, language patterns and picture clues helped children to predict the monkeys' actions in *Caps of Many Colors* and what fish would appear in *In the Big Blue Sea*. Prior knowledge of Norbert Wu's work, along with picture clues, helped them to predict the answer to the title question *What Do You Do, Norbert Wu?* After looking at each selection, help children develop a one- or two-sentence summary of it.

TARGET SKILL
BUILDING FLUENCY
Storytelling

Revisit Familiar Texts Review the **Phonics Library** story "Look at Me!" Remind children that they've been learning about words with initial *m*. As they retell the **Phonics Library** story "Look at Me!" have them look for /m/ pictures.

Review Feature several familiar Phonics Library titles in the Book Corner. Have children demonstrate their growing skills by choosing one to describe the pictures, alternating pages with a partner.

Oral Language Frequent retellings of familiar texts help children grow more confident in their oral language. Model adding details to a story and speaking with expression. Then have children try it.

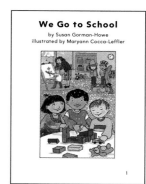

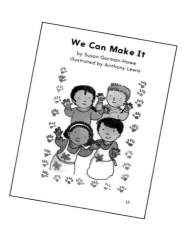

Books for Small-Group Reading

The materials listed below provide reading practice for children at different levels.

Vocabulary Reader

Leveled Reader

Little Big Book

Little Readers for Guided Reading

Houghton Mifflin Classroom Bookshelf

Home Connection
Remind children to share the take-home version of "Look at Me!" with their families.

OBJECTIVES

- Review initial consonants *m, s*.
- Review letter names.
- Make sentences with high-frequency words.

Materials

- **Word Cards** *I, see*
- **Picture Cards** for *m, s*; choose others for sentence building
- **Punctuation Card** period

PHONICS

Initial Consonants: *m, s*

❶ Review

Review identifying initial consonants *m, s*. Tell children that they will take turns naming pictures and telling what letter stands for the beginning sound.

- Randomly place four **Picture Cards** along the chalkboard ledge and write *m* and *s* on the board.

- Call on four children to come up and stand in front of a **Picture Card**. In turn, have each child name the picture, say the initial sound, and point to *m* or *s*.

- Have the rest of the class verify that the correct letter has been chosen. Then write the picture name on the board and underline the initial consonant.

- Continue until everyone has a chance to name a picture and point to the consonant that stands for its beginning sound.

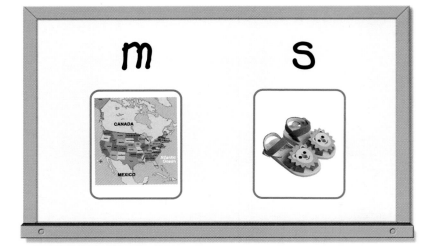

HIGH-FREQUENCY WORDS
I, see

❷ Review

Review the high-frequency words *I, see*.

- Give each small group the **Word Cards, Picture Cards,** and **Punctuation Card** needed to make a sentence. Each child holds one card.

- Children stand and arrange themselves to make a sentence for others to read.

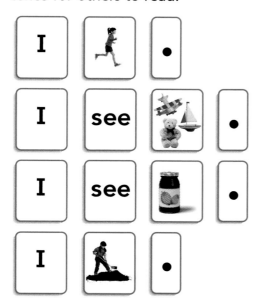

❸ Practice/Apply

- Children can complete **Practice Book** page 89 independently and read it to you during small group time.

- Pass out copies of **Practice Book** page 197–198, *I See* 🍽️. Read the title aloud.

- Ask children to tell who is speaking. Point to the character and tell children that the boy is telling the story.

- For each page, have children look at the picture and predict what the boy will see. Have them read the sentences silently. Then have a child read the page aloud. Use questions such as the following to prompt discussion:

    Pages 1–4 What is the family getting ready to do? What do you like to do to help get ready for breakfast? What is each family member having for breakfast?

- Then have children count the high-frequency words in the story: How many times can you find the word *I* in this story? the word *see*?

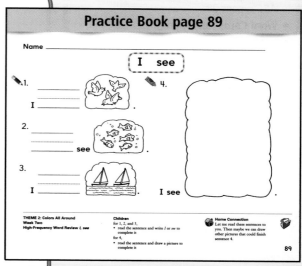

Practice Book page 89

Practice Book pages 197–198

Monitoring Student Progress

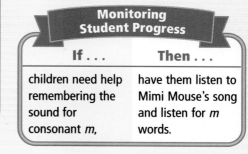

If . . .	Then . . .
children need help remembering the sound for consonant *m*,	have them listen to Mimi Mouse's song and listen for *m* words.

High-Frequency Words   **T127**

OBJECTIVES

- Explore color words.

Materials

- *From Apples to Zebras: A Book of ABC's,* page 29
- **Word Cards** color words

EXPLORING WORDS
Color Words

Match colors to words.

- Display page 29 of *From Apples to Zebras: A Book of ABC's.* Call on children to point to and name the colors on the page.

- Then distribute the **Word Cards**. Call on children to match the **Word Cards** to the color words on the page.

- Discuss the colors with children. What other words have you learned that help to name the color red? the color green?

Discuss and identify colors of fish.

- Have children recall the colors of the fish they read about in *In the Big Blue Sea.* What fish colors surprised you? What color fish have you seen?

- Invite children to create a fish of their own design. Tell children that the fish can be any color they choose. The fish can also have stripes, spots, or other designs on them.

- Have children draw or paint their fish. When the drawings are finished, children can share their drawings and describe the fish by color.

INDEPENDENT WRITING
Journals

Preparing to Write

- Direct attention to this week's Shared and Interactive Writing activities posted in the classroom. (See pages T113 and T121.) Have children read the writing samples.

- Point out the different color words children used. Tell children that today they will write in their journals about something they learned.

Writing Independently

- Pass out the journals.

- *Let's discuss some of the things we read about this week. What did the man sell in* Caps of Many Colors? *What did Norbert Wu take pictures of in* In the Big Blue Sea? *What can you tell me about Norbert Wu's job?*

- Tell children that they will now have a chance to write about something they did this week. Children might write about their favorite fish in *In the Big Blue Sea* or write and draw about a picture they would like to take.

- As children write, remind them that they can use the words on the Word Wall and those posted in the Writing and Science Centers for help in writing words.

- If time permits, have children share what they've written with the class.

clownfish

brown bear

Portfolio Opportunity

Mark journal entries you would like to share with parents. Allow children to indicate their best efforts or favorite works for sharing as well.

REACHING ALL LEARNERS

English Language Learners

Children may have difficulty writing by themselves. Have them work in small groups to create one descriptive sentence each, which can be copied into their journals.

LEVELED READERS

WEEK 2

Look at Me!

Summary: *This story is about a girl getting ready to go outside on a rainy day. Readers see and read about all her clothing and gear, including socks, boots, sweater, coat, hat, and umbrella. At last, the girl is ready for the rainy weather. Dressed in her rainy day outfit, she is happily standing in the rain.*

Story Words

Look *p. 2*

at *p. 2*

my *p. 2*

Building Background and Vocabulary

Begin discussing this story by explaining that this book is about the clothes a girl needs to wear to go outside on a rainy day. Look through the illustrations with children. Encourage children to talk about what they wear to go outside on a rainy day. Then ask children whether or not they enjoy rainy weather. Have them give reasons for their opinions.

⊚ Comprehension Skill: Inferences: Making Predictions

Read together the Strategy Focus on the book flap. Remind children, as they read, to look at the pictures and think about what they will see next in the story.

Responding

Discussing the Book Encourage children to share their responses to the book. Ask them to talk about what they liked best about the book. Have children compare their own rainy day gear to the items worn by the girl in the story. Then direct children's attention to the bright colors on each page. Ask volunteers to point to each illustration and tell the color of that item.

Responding Have children answer the questions on the inside back cover. Then help them complete the Writing and Drawing activity. Have children take turns sharing their drawings with classmates and explaining why they wear that specific item on a rainy day.

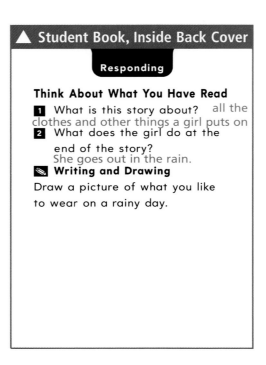

▲ Student Book, Inside Back Cover

Responding

Think About What You Have Read

1 What is this story about? all the clothes and other things a girl puts on

2 What does the girl do at the end of the story? She goes out in the rain.

✎ **Writing and Drawing**

Draw a picture of what you like to wear on a rainy day.

Building Fluency

Model Have children follow along as you reread pages 2 and 3 to them. Point out that the first three words, *Look at my,* on the two pages are the same. Tell children that these words begin every page in the book except for the last page. Turn to page 8 together. Read that page aloud for children and ask them to tell what new word is on that page.

Practice Divide the class into two groups. For each page, have one group read the repeating phrase, *Look at my*, while the other group reads the word that tells the item seen in the picture. Have both groups read the last page together.

Oral Language Development

Color Words Explain that color words are words that tell the color of things. Page through the book with children, asking children to name the item or items they see in the pictures. Ask volunteers to name the color of each thing shown in the picture (*brown socks, red boots, green sweater, yellow coat, pink hat, blue umbrella*).

Practice Have children practice using the color words by naming other things that are the same color as each item shown in the illustrations. Encourage children to draw pictures of the things they name and label each picture with the correct color word.

Lesson Overview

Literature

HOUGHTON MIFFLIN
Reading

I Went Walking

WRITTEN BY
Sue Williams

ILLUSTRATED BY
Julie Vivas

Includes:
Science Link

HOUGHTON MIFFLIN
Reading

In the Big Blue Sea

by Chyng Feng Sun
Photography by Norbert Wu

Includes:
Science Link

1 **Teacher Read Aloud**

• *How the Birds Got Their Colors*

2 **Big Books**

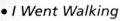

• *I Went Walking*
• *In the Big Blue Sea*

3 **Wordless Book**

Phonics Library

• "The Parade"

The Parade
by Susan Gorman-Howe
illustrated by Joan Paley

4 **Science and Social Studies Links**

These Links appear after the main Big Book selections.

T130

Leveled Books

Vocabulary Reader

- Below Level, ELL
- Lesson

Leveled Reader

- On Level, Above Level
- Lesson
- Take-Home Version

Plus!
Online Leveled Books

Instructional Support

Planning and Practice

Tennessee Teacher's Edition

Alphafriends

Teacher's Resources

Practice book

Ready-Made Centers

Phonics Center

Building Vocabulary

Reading in Science and Social Studies
- 30 books and activities
- support for Tennessee content standards

Hands-On Literacy Centers for Week 3
- activities
- manipulatives
- routines

Differentiated Instruction

Intervention/Extra Support

English Language Learners

Challenge

Technology

Audio Selections
I Went Walking

In the Big Blue Sea

Curious George **Learns Phonics**

www.eduplace.com
- over 1,000 Online Leveled Books

Daily Lesson Plans

 Technology

Lesson Planner CD-ROM allows you to customize the chart below to develop your own lesson plans.

T Skill tested on Weekly or Theme Skills Test and/or Integrated Theme Test

 Tennessee Curriculum Standards indicated in blue.

<table>

WEEK 3 — DAILY LESSON PLANS

60–90 minutes

Learning to Read

Phonemic Awareness

Phonics

High–Frequency Words

Comprehension

Concepts of Print

Vocabulary Reader
Birds

FRUIT

Leveled Reader

DAY 1

K.1.01.g, K.1.02.b, K.1.06.a
Daily Routines, *T138–T139*
Calendar, Message, High-Frequency Words

 Phonemic Awareness T K.1.04.f, K.1.04.g

Teacher Read Aloud, *T140–T143*

 Comprehension Strategy, *T140* K.1.08.c
Predict/Infer

 Comprehension Skill, *T140* K.1.09.b.1
Sequence of Events **T**

 Phonemic Awareness, *T144–T145* K.1.04.f
Beginning Sound /r/ **T**

Cross-Curricular Activity, T137 SC.K.5.2

Leveled Reader
K.1.06, K.1.07, K.1.09.a

DAY 2

K.1.02.b, K.3.02.e, K.1.06.a
Daily Routines, *T148–T149*
Calendar, Message, High-Frequency Words

 Phonemic Awareness T K.1.04.f, K.1.04.g

Reading the Big Book, *T150–T151*

 Comprehension Strategy, *T150* K.1.08.c
Predict/Infer

 Comprehension Skill, *T150* K.1.08.c
Inferences: Making Predictions **T**

 Phonics, *T152–T153* K.1.04.f
Initial Consonant *r* **T**

 High-Frequency Word, *T154–T155* K.1.0...
Review Words: *I, see* **T**

 Word and Picture Book, *T155*
K.1.01.e, K.1.13.a, K.1.12.a

Leveled Reader
K.1.06, K.1.07, K.1.09.a

30–45 minutes

Word Work

High-Frequency Word Practice

Exploring Words

DAY 1

High-Frequency Word Practice, *T146* K.1.06.a
Words: *I, see*

DAY 2

High-Frequency Word Practice, *T156* K.3.0...
K.2.1...
Building Sentences

30–45 minutes

Writing and Oral Language

Vocabulary

Writing

Listening/Speaking/ Viewing

DAY 1

 Oral Language: Vocabulary, *T147*
Using Singular and Plural Words K.1.01.a, K.1.07.a

Vocabulary Reader K.1.07.a

DAY 2

Vocabulary Reader K.1.07.a

 Vocabulary Expansion, *T157*
Using Plural Names K.1.01.a, K.1.07.a

Listening/Speaking/Viewing, *T157*
K.1.01.g, K.1.02.b

</table>

 Half-Day Kindergarten

Focus on lessons for tested skills marked with **T**.
Then choose other activities as time allows.

Target Skills of the Week

Phonemic Awareness	Beginning Sounds; Words in Oral Sentences
Phonics	Initial Consonant: *Rr*
Comprehension	Sequence of Events; Making Predictions; Summarize
Vocabulary	High-Frequency Words; Color, Singular/Plural Words
Fluency	Phonics Library; Word and Picture Book; Practice Reader

---

DAY 3

K.1.02.a, K.2.02.a, K.1.06.a

Daily Routines, *T158–T159*
Calendar, Message,
High-Frequency Words

Phonemic Awareness **T** K.1.04.f, K.1.04.g

Reading the Big Book, *T160–T161*

Comprehension Strategy, *T160*
Summarize K.1.09.b.2

Comprehension Skill, *T160* K.1.08.c
Inferences: Making Predictions **T**

Phonics, *T162* K.1.04.f
Initial Consonant *r* **T**

Storytelling Practice, *T163–T165*
"The Parade" K.1.13.a, K.1.04.f, K.1.08.d,
K.1.09.b.2, K.1.09.b.4

Vocabulary Reader K.1.07.a

Leveled Reader
K.1.06, K.1.07, K.1.09.a

Exploring Words, *T166* K.1.07.a, K.1.01.e
Color Words

Shared Writing, *T167* K.2.01.c
Writing a Graphic Organizer

DAY 4

K.1.01.g, K.1.04.f, K.1.06.a

Daily Routines, *T168–T169*
Calendar, Message,
High-Frequency Words

Phonemic Awareness **T** K.1.04.f, K.1.04.g

Reading the Links:
What's My Favorite Color, T170
What Do You Do, Norbert Wu?, T171

Comprehension Strategy, *T170–T171*
Predict/Infer; Summarize K.1.08.c, K.1.09.b.2

Comprehension Skill, *T170–T171*
Making Predictions; Sequence of Events **T**
K.1.08.c, K.1.09.b.1

Concepts of Print, *T170–T171*
Capitalize First Word in Sentence;
End Punctuation **T** K.3.02.d, K.3.02.e

Phonics, *T172–T173* K.1.04.f
Initial Consonant *r* **T**

Vocabulary Reader K.1.07.a

Leveled Reader
K.1.06, K.1.07, K.1.09.a

Exploring Words, *T174* K.1.03.b, K.1.07.a
Color Words

Interactive Writing, *T175* K.2.02.b
Writing a Class Story

DAY 5

K.1.01.g, K.3.02.d,
K.3.02.e, K.1.04.e

Daily Routines, *TT176–T177*
Calendar, Message,
High-Frequency Words

Phonemic Awareness **T** K.1.04.f, K.1.04.g

Revisiting the Literature, *T178*

Comprehension Skill, *T178*
Making Predictions; Sequence of Events **T**
K.1.08.c, K.1.09.b.1

On My Way Practice Reader, *T179*
Animal Colors K.1.03.e, K.1.08.a, K.1.12.

Phonics Review, *T180* K.1.04.f
Initial Consonants: *r, m, s* **T**

High-Frequency Word Review, *T181*
Words: *I, see* **T** K.1.06.a

Word and Picture Book, *T181*
K.1.01.e, K.1.13.a, K.1.12.a

Vocabulary Reader K.1.07.a

Leveled Reader
K.1.06, K.1.07, K.1.09.a

Exploring Words, *T182* K.1.07
Color Words

Independent Writing, *T183* K.2.11.a
Journals

Concepts of Print lessons teach important foundational skills for Phonics.

Managing Flexible Groups

WHOLE CLASS

DAY 1

- Daily Routines (TE pp. T138–T139)
- Teacher Read Aloud: *How the Birds Got Their Colors* (TE pp. T140–T143)
- Phonemic Awareness (TE pp. T144–T145)

DAY 2

- Daily Routines (TE pp. T148–T149)
- Big Book: *I Went Walking* (TE pp. T150–T151)
- Phonics lesson (TE pp. T152–T153)
- High-Frequency Word lesson (TE pp. T154–T155)

SMALL GROUPS

Organize small groups according to children's needs.

DAY 1

TEACHER-LED GROUPS

- Begin Practice Book pp. 91, 92, 93, 94. (TE pp. T141, T145)
- Introduce Phonics Center. (TE p. T145)
- Leveled Reader

DAY 2

TEACHER-LED GROUPS

- Begin Practice Book p. 95. (TE p. T153)
- Write letters *R, r*; begin handwriting Blackline Master 174 or 200. (TE p. T153)
- Introduce Phonics Center. (TE p. T153)
- Leveled Reader
- Vocabulary Reader

INDEPENDENT GROUPS

- Complete Practice Book pp. 91, 92, 93, 94. (TE pp. T141, T145)
- Use Phonics Center. (TE p. T144)

INDEPENDENT GROUPS

- Complete Practice Book p. 95. (TE p. T153)
- Complete Blackline Master 174 or 200.
- Use Phonics Center. (TE p. T153)
- **Fluency Practice** Read Word and Picture Book: *I See* . (Practice Book pp. 199–200)

English Language Learners Support is provided in the Reaching All Learners notes throughout the week.

Independent Activities

- Complete Practice Book pages 91–98.
- Complete penmanship practice (Teacher's Resource Blackline Master 174 or 200).
- Retell familiar Phonics Library stories or reread Word and Picture Books.
- Share trade books from Leveled Bibliography. (See pp. T4–T5)

DAY 3

- Daily Routines (TE pp. T158–T159)
- Big Book: *In the Big Blue Sea* (TE pp. T160–T161)
- Phonics lesson (TE p. T162)

TEACHER-LED GROUPS

- Begin Practice Book p. 96. (TE p. T161)
- Tell Phonics Library: "The Parade." (TE pp. T163–T165)
- Leveled Reader
- Vocabulary Reader

INDEPENDENT GROUPS

- Complete Practice Book p. 96. (TE p. T161)
- **Fluency Practice** Retell Phonics Library: "The Parade." (TE pp. T163–T165)

DAY 4

- Daily Routines (TE pp. T168–T169)
- Science Link: *What's My Favorite Color?* (TE p. T170)
- Science Link: *What Do You Do, Norbert Wu?* (TE p. T171)
- Phonics lesson (TE pp. T172–T173)

TEACHER-LED GROUPS

- Begin Practice Book p. 97. (TE p. T173)
- Introduce the Phonics Center. (TE p. T173)
- **Fluency Practice** Reread Word and Picture Book: *I See* .
- Leveled Reader
- Vocabulary Reader

INDEPENDENT GROUPS

- Complete Practice Book p. 97. (TE p. T173)
- **Fluency Practice** Color and retell Phonics Library: "The Parade." (TE pp. T163–T165)
- Use Phonics Center. (TE p. T173)

DAY 5

- Daily Routines (TE pp. T176–T177)
- Retelling (TE p. T178)
- On My Way Practice Reader (TE p. T179)
- Phonics and High-Frequency Word Review (TE pp. T180–T181)

TEACHER-LED GROUPS

- Read Word and Practice Book *I See* .
- Begin Practice Book pp. 98. (TE p. T181)
- **Fluency Practice** Retell the Take-Home version of "The Parade."
- Leveled Reader
- Vocabulary Reader

INDEPENDENT GROUPS

- Complete Practice Book p. 98. (TE p. T181)
- **Fluency Practice** Reread Word and Practice Book *I See* . Retell a favorite Phonics Library or Leveled Reader story.

- Retell or reread Little Big Books.
- Listen to Big Book Audio CDs.
- Use the Phonics Center and other Centers. (See pp. T136–T137)

Turn the page for more independent activities.

Managing Flexible Groups   **T135**

MADE FOR TENNESSEE

Building Vocabulary

ELA.K.1.01.a, ELA.K.1.01.e,
ELA.K.1.01.f, ELA.K.1.01.g,
ELA.K.1.07.a, ELA.K.1.07.b

Center Activity 6

Building Vocabulary
Center Activity 6
In the Big Blue Sea

2 Learn from Context — Small Groups — Connect to Science

Smell the Roses
The fish in the story come in many pretty colors. Flowers do, too. Learn about a special flower.

1 Read the Words

Vocabulary Link
color

New Words

rose a pretty flower with a sweet smell

petal the soft, colorful part of a flower

stem the thin part of a plant that holds the flower

leaf the flat green part of the plant near the flower

vase a type of jar to hold water

petal
leaf
stem
vase
rose

3 Do an Activity

Leveled Activities on back of card	● Below Level ▲ On Level ■ Above Level

Hands-On Literacy Centers

Challenge and Routine Cards

Drawing Letters
Materials
gAzQ
1 Choose a letter.
2 Say the name.
3 Touch and trace.

Share
Tell a friend.

1. Fishing Game
Go fishing for m, r, and s fish.

Manipulatives

I

Reading in Science

Independent Book
A Walk in the Woods
Students apply comprehension skills to nonfiction text.

SC.K.5.2, ELA.K.1.11.b

Center Activity 6

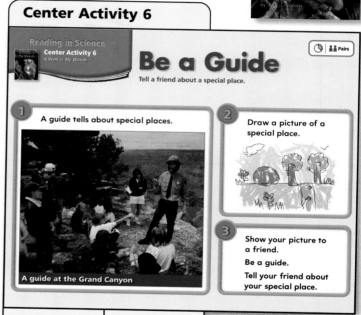

Reading in Science
Center Activity 6
A Walk in My Woods

Pairs

Be a Guide
Tell a friend about a special place.

1 A guide tells about special places.

A guide at the Grand Canyon

2 Draw a picture of a special place.

3 Show your picture to a friend.
Be a guide.
Tell your friend about your special place.

Leveled Activities on back of card	● Below Level ▲ On Level ■ Above Level

More Nonfiction Reading

30 topics aligned with Tennessee Science and Social Studies standards!

Setting Up Centers

Writing Center

Materials
singular and plural words chart from Day 1

Children draw several pictures based on the chart. Then children use their knowledge of consonants and initial sounds to label their pictures. See page T147 for this week's Writing Center activity.

Science Center

Materials
Blackline Masters 39–40, sea animals and animal picture books, markers, drawing paper

Gather the picture books about the sea early in the week. Children draw animals on Blackline Masters 39–40. They also draw sea creatures. Later in the week children draw and sort pictures of fruit. See pages T151, T161, and T171 for the activities.

SC.K.5.2

Art Center

Materials
drawing paper, water color or tempera paints

Children draw and label pictures of their favorite animals from I Went Walking. See page T157 for this week's Art Center activity.

Day at a Glance
T138–T147

Learning to Read

Teacher Read Aloud, *T140*
Phonemic Awareness: /r/, *T144*

Word Work

High Frequency Word Practice,
T146

Writing & Oral Language

Oral Language, *T147*

Daily Routines

Sunday	Monday	Tuesday	Wednesday	Thursday	Friday	Saturday
			1	2	3	4
5	6	7	8	9	10	11
12	13	14	15	16	17	18
19	20	21	22	23	24	25
26	27	28	29	30	31	

Calendar

Reading the Calendar To begin the new week, ask a child to find today's date on the calendar. Then review the days of the week. Together count the number of days left in the month.

Daily Message

Modeled Writing
Incorporate the colors of children's clothing into the daily message.

> Sean has a canary yellow shirt. Kristen has a cardinal red dress. Today we'll read how the birds got their colors.

Word Wall

Ask children to find and read the word they added to the Word Wall last week. Then chant the spelling of the words on the Word Wall with children: *s-e-e* spells *see*; capital *I* spells *I*, capital *I* spells *I*

I	see

Word Cards for these words appear on page R8.

Daily Phonemic Awareness

Beginning Sounds

- Tell children that they will play a listening game. I will say three words. Two of the words will begin with the same sound. Listen carefully for words that begin with the same sound: *pan, pull, dish*. Yes, *pan* and *pull* begin with the same sound, /p/.

- Say the following words, emphasizing each beginning sound: *nose, head, neck*. When most hands are up, call on children to identify the two words that begin with the same sound. Continue with these words: *soap, seven, fan; jam, jet, bug; came, hat, hand*.

Words in Oral Sentences

- Read "I Love Colors" on page 10 of *Higglety Pigglety*.

- Say: Sentences are made up of words. I am going to read a sentence. I'll make a mark on the board for each word. *I love colors, yes I do!*

- Have children clap and count the words. Repeat with other sentences. How many words did you hear?

Higglety Pigglety: A Book of Rhymes, page 10

To help children plan their day, tell them that they will—

- listen to a story called *How the Birds Got Their Colors*.

- meet a new Alphafriend.

- act out a story in the Dramatic Play Center.

OBJECTIVES

- Develop oral language (listening, responding).
- Preview comprehension skill.

Read Aloud

How the Birds Got Their Colors

Selection Summary In this porquoi tale, Rascal Raccoon covers Wolf's eyes with mud while he is napping. When Wolf awakes, he can't see. Fortunately, the woodland birds peck the hardened mud from his eyes. To thank them, Wolf paints them different colors. He then forgives Raccoon and paints her a mischievous mask.

Key Concept Colors of birds

REACHING ALL LEARNERS
English Language Learners

Before reading, share picture books on birds to familiarize children with the birds mentioned in the selection. You may want to point out birds common to your area.

Teacher Read Aloud

Building Background

Have children describe some of the birds they have seen. Guide the discussion so they talk about brightly colored birds as well as those that have markings such as spots, stripes, and speckles.

- As you display the illustration, tell children that today's story is a pourquoi tale, a story that tells how something happened. Explain that this tale came from North and South America and tells how the birds got their colors.

TARGET SKILL
COMPREHENSION STRATEGY
Predict/Infer

Teacher Modeling Remind children that good readers think about what a story will be about. They make predictions about what will happen, and then as they read they check to see if their predictions were correct.

- Look at the illustration. What do you think this story is about? Do you see birds in the picture? What colors are they? What else is in the picture? As we read, we'll check our predictions.

TARGET SKILL
COMPREHENSION SKILL
Sequence of Events

Teacher Modeling Remind children that good readers try to remember what happens at the beginning of a story, in the middle, and at the end. Doing this helps them remember the order of events. Often the beginning is where you find out the problem. Ask: What is the problem in this story?

Listening to the Story

Fold your Teacher's Edition so that children can see page T143 as you read. Note that the art is also available on the back of the Theme Poster.

As you read the story aloud, pause at the discussion points so that children can sequence the events. Later, on a rereading, point out descriptive phrases such as . . . *hear the wind dancing through the trees* and . . . *rushed to his side in a great cloud of feathers.*

Responding

Oral Language: Summarizing the Story   Help children summarize parts of the story.

- What happened at the beginning of the story? Why did Raccoon put mud over Wolf's eyes?

- What happened when Wolf woke up? How did the birds help him?

- What did Wolf do after his eyes were clear again?

- What did Wolf do at the end of the story?

- What was your favorite part of the story?

Practice Book   Children will complete **Practice Book** pages 91–92 during small group time.

Practice Book page 91

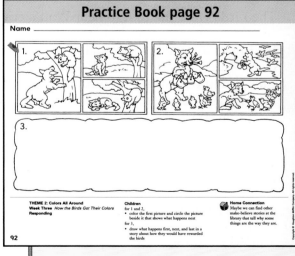

Practice Book page 92

Dramatic Play Center

Materials   paper lunch bags • colored markers • colored paper

Prepare large paper-bag puppets for Wolf and Raccoon. Children make lunch-bag sized puppets for the birds. One side of the paper bag can show a gray bird; the other side a brightly colored or patterned bird. Children can use the puppets to act out the story and take turns playing the roles of Wolf and Raccoon.

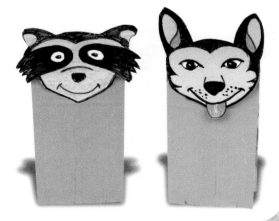

How the Birds Got Their Colors

A Pourquoi Tale Told in North and South America

How did the birds get their colors? Have you ever wondered about that? Some folks say the birds can thank the wolf for their beautiful colors.

Long ago, all the birds and animals in the forest shared and helped one another. One of the strongest and most helpful of them all was Wolf. He was the fastest runner and best hunter, and he always shared what he had. Raccoon shared too, but she was mischievous, so it was mostly pranks and tricks that she shared. She was such a troublemaker in fact, that everyone called her Rascal Raccoon.

One day Rascal Raccoon annoyed Wolf so much that he chased her up a tree. With Raccoon up in the tree, Wolf decided to take a nap. When Wolf was sound asleep, Raccoon crept down the tree. "Now is my chance to play a great trick on Wolf," she thought.

So Raccoon set to work scooping mud from the soft, wet ground. She spread it over Wolf's eyes, where it dried, hard as clay. Then she hid nearby to see what would happen. **(Ask: What happened to Rascal Raccoon first on this day? What did she do next? After that?)**

Soon Wolf began to stretch and yawn. He could hear the wind dancing through the trees, and he could smell the scent of wildflowers. But when he tried to open his great green eyes, it was dark!

"O-w-o-o-o," howled Wolf. "I cannot see. What will become of me?" **(Ask: Why can't Wolf see? Do you think anyone will help him?)**

The birds were the first to hear Wolf's cries. They rushed to his side in a great cloud of feathers. It was hard to tell one bird from another because all the birds were the same color—dull gray. The birds looked closely at Wolf; soon they found out what was wrong. Rascal Raccoon was rolling with laughter as she watched. She had never seen anything so silly.

At last Wise Old Owl called for silence. "I have an idea," he said. "We can peck the mud from Wolf's eyes." The birds pecked carefully because they didn't want to hurt their friend. After many hours, Wolf's great green eyes finally opened wide again. "Thank you, thank you, my little feathered friends," he called. "How can I repay your kindness? I will do anything I can for you."

All the birds thought and thought, until, finally, a tiny gray hummingbird spoke up. "Please, Wolf," begged Hummingbird, "we don't like being dull and gray. The wildflowers and butterflies are such beautiful colors. We were wondering if you could make all of us bright colors too."

"That's a wonderful idea!" exclaimed Wolf. "I'll see what I can do." So he got some paint pots from his den. Then he set about making some brilliant colors. He used purple from berries, red from roses, yellow from marigolds, and green from leaves. Wolf mixed the colors and sprinkled little flecks of gold from the sun over all.

When Wolf was ready, Cardinal flew to the front of the line, asking to be the first to get his new color. Wolf painted him a bright red color. Next came a small finch. Wolf painted him gold and black. "From now on," said Wolf, "you will be known as Goldfinch!"

The jay was painted blue and white and black. Now he would be called Blue Jay. The hummingbird was painted bright green and the mallard's colors were shiny and dark. Wolf gave Woodpecker stripes, spots, and a red head, and Owl got speckles. One by one, the birds flew off to brighten the forest with their new colors.

At last, Wolf sat back, tired but happy. Then he felt a tap on his shoulder. And there, looking a bit sad and sorry, was Rascal Raccoon. **(Ask: What do you think Raccoon will say and do? Why?)**

"Please, Wolf," Raccoon asked, "will you forgive me? I'm sorry I played a trick on you. I saw how kind the birds were to you and the reward you gave them in return."

"I forgive you," said Wolf slowly, "if you promise not to tease anyone."

"Oh, I promise," answered Raccoon quickly. "But I want to ask a favor of you. Will you paint me too?"

The paint in Wolf's pots was almost gone, but he had some lovely black and brown left. So he used that to paint rings around Raccoon's tail. And then—just for fun—he painted a black mask around Raccoon's eyes. When Raccoon looked at her reflection in the pond, she was very pleased.

So that's one story about how birds got the bright colors they wear today. And when you see a raccoon, you'll remember the story about how it got a ringed tail and black mask. **(Say: For awhile, Wolf couldn't see. Who helped him? What did Wolf do next? Do you think this is a story that could really happen?)**

OBJECTIVES

- Identify pictures whose names begin with /r/.

Materials

- **Alphafriend Cards** *Mimi Mouse, Reggie Rooster, Sammy Seal*
- **Alphafriend CD** Theme 2
- **Alphafolder** *Reggie Rooster*
- **Picture Cards** *man, map, mop, rock, rope, rug, salt, sandals, sun*
- **Phonics Center** Theme 2, Week 3, Day 1

Alphafolder *Reggie Rooster*

 Home Connection

Hand out the take-home version of Reggie Rooster's Song. Ask children to share the song with their families. (See **Alphafriends Blackline Masters**.)

 English Language Learners

Because the English *r* is different from most *r* sounds in other languages, many children have difficulty pronouncing the /r/ sound. Display **Picture Cards** for *r.* Then name each picture with children.

 PHONEMIC AWARENESS
Beginning Sound

❶ Teach

Introduce Alphafriend: Reggie Rooster
Use the Alphafriend routine to introduce Reggie Rooster.

▶ **Alphafriend Riddle** Read these clues:

- Our new Alphafriend's sound is /r/. Say it with me: /r/.
- This feathered animal has a *rrred* cap on his head.
- He *rrrules* the barnyard and the *rrroost*.
- He wakes up the whole farm with a "cock-a-doodle-doo."

When most hands are up, call on children until they name *rooster*.

▶ **Pocket Chart** Display Reggie Rooster in a pocket chart. Explain that Reggie's sound is /r/. Say his name, stretching the /r/ sound slightly, and have children echo this.

▶ **Alphafriend CD** Play Reggie Rooster's song. Listen for /r/ words in Reggie's song.

▶ **Alphafolder** Have children find the /r/ pictures in the scene.

▶ **Summarize**

- What is our Alphafriend's name? What is his sound?
- What words in our Alphafriend's song start with /r/?
- Each time you look at Reggie Rooster this week, remember the /r/ sound.

Reggie Rooster's Song

(tune: Hush! Little Baby)

Reggie has a rocket that is red.

Reggie keeps it right beside his bed.

Reggie likes to listen to rock 'n roll.

Reggie plays it on his radio.

❷ Guided Practice

Listen for /r/ and compare and review /m/ and /s/. Display Alphafriends *Mimi Mouse* and *Sammy Seal* opposite *Reggie Rooster*. Review each character's sound.

Name some pictures. Have children signal "thumbs up" for each one that starts with Reggie Rooster's sound, /r/. Have children put the card below Reggie's picture. For "thumbs down" words, have them put cards below the correct Alphafriends.

Pictures: *man, map, mop, rock, rope, rug, salt, sandals, sun*

Tell children they will sort more pictures in the **Phonics Center** today.

❸ Apply

Have children complete **Practice Book** pages 93–94 at small group time.

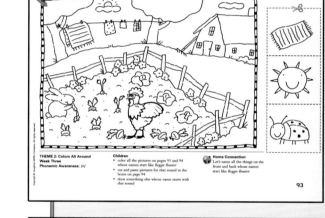

Practice Book page 93

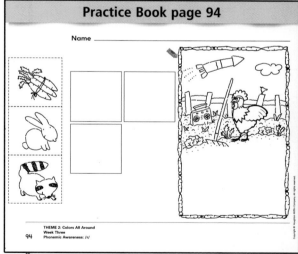

Practice Book page 94

ABC **Phonics Center**

Materials Phonics Center materials for Theme 2, Week 3, Day 1 ·

Display Day 1 Direction Chart. Children put *Reggie Rooster* (without letter) in separate sections of Workmat 2. Then they sort remaining pictures by initial sound: /r/ and not /r/.

OBJECTIVES

- Read high-frequency words.
- Create and write sentences with high-frequency words.

Materials

- *Higglety Pigglety: A Book of Rhymes,* page 38
- **Word Cards** *I, see*
- **Picture Cards** *berries, red, sandals, toys*
- **Punctuation Card** period

PRACTICE

High-Frequency Words

Display Word Cards for the high-frequency words *I* and *see* in a pocket chart.

- Have children read each word and match it on the Word Wall.

- Remind children that these words are often found in books. I'll read a poem. You listen to hear if these words are used in it.

- Read the poem "Tommy" on page 38 of *Higglety Pigglety.* Did you hear the words *I* and *see* in the poem? Let's see if you can match the Word Cards *I* and *see* to the words *I* and *see* in the poem.

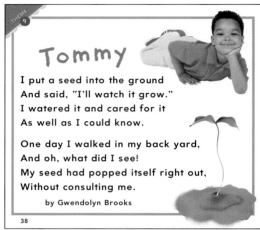

THEME 9

Tommy

I put a seed into the ground
And said, "I'll watch it grow."
I watered it and cared for it
As well as I could know.

One day I walked in my back yard,
And oh, what did I see!
My seed had popped itself right out,
Without consulting me.

by Gwendolyn Brooks

38

Higglety Pigglety: A Book of Rhymes, page 38

Have children write sentences.

- Place the **Word Cards** *I see* in a pocket chart as a sentence stem.

- Then display the **Picture Cards** *berries, red, sandals,* and *toys.* Help children build sentences with the cards.

- Children can write and illustrate one of the sentences or use the words to create their own sentences with rebus pictures.

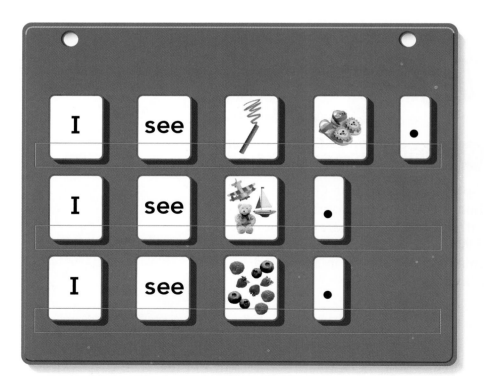

ORAL LANGUAGE: VOCABULARY
Using Singular and Plural Words

OBJECTIVES
- Use singular and plural nouns.

Materials
- **Read Aloud** *How the Birds Got Their Colors*

① Teach

Discuss singular and plural naming words.

- Remind children that some words are nouns, or naming words. These words name people, places, and things.

- Display *How the Birds Got Their Colors.* Use naming words to tell me what you see in the picture.

- Write children's responses on chart paper, listing singular nouns in one column and plural nouns in another.

- What do you notice about the words in the second column? Explain that some naming words name one person or one thing, while others name more than one person or thing. We add the letter *s* or sometimes *es* to a naming word to mean "more than one."

② Practice/Apply

Have children practice using singular and plural naming words. Continue to page through the book and ask children to use naming words to tell what they see in the pictures. List children's responses.

One	More Than One
raccoon	birds
wolf	branches
tree	trees

✏ Writing Center

Materials drawing paper • crayons and markers

Place the chart in the Writing Center. Tell children to draw a picture of one person, animal, or object on one half of the paper. On the other half, they will draw more than one person, animal, or object. Encourage children to label their pictures, using what they know about letters and their sounds. Remind children they can also refer to charts, labels, the Word Wall, and books as they write.

English Language Learners

Most children will not have problems adding *s* to form plural nouns, but they may be confused that the article stays the same. Help children to name and label their pictures accordingly, for example: *the bird; the birds.*

DAY 2
week 3

Day at a Glance
T148–T157

Learning to Read

Big Book, *T150*
Phonics: Initial Consonant *r, T152*
High Frequency Words: *I, see,*
T154

Word Work

High Frequency Word Practice,
T156

Writing &
Oral Language

Vocabulary Expansion, *T157*

Daily Routines

Sunday	Monday	Tuesday	Wednesday	Thursday	Friday	Saturday
			1	2	3	4
5	6	7	8	9	10	11
12	13	14	15	16	17	18
19	20	21	22	23	24	25
26	27	28	29	30	31	

Calendar

Reading the Calendar Find today's date on the calendar with the children. Count how many more school days there are in the week. Talk about special events that will occur soon.

Daily Message

Modeled Writing As you write the daily message, model for children what you are doing: The first word in a sentence begins with a capital letter. The first word in my sentence is *today,* so I will begin writing with a capital *T.*

Today we will go outside at 10:30.

Word Wall

Have children find and read the words they've added to the Word Wall. Chant the spellings with children. Then have individuals use the words in complete oral sentences.

I	see

Word Cards for these words appear on page R8.

Daily Phonemic Awareness

Beginning Sounds

- Read "Rainy Day" on page 13 of *Higglety Pigglety*. Tell children that they will play What's the Sound? I will say a word from the poem. You listen for the beginning sound and tell me the sound you hear. Now listen: *rrrainy*. When most hands are up, have children voice the sound. Yes, /r/ is the beginning sound of *rainy*.

- Continue with other words from the poem: *like, wet, wish, road*.

Words in Oral Sentences

- Remind children that sentences are made up of words. Tell them to clap for each word they hear in this sentence: *The sun is warm and bright*. How many claps did you hear?

- Repeat the sentence, making a tally mark on the board for each word. Have children count the tally marks to check their answers.

Rainy Day

I do not like a rainy day.
The road is wet, the sky is gray.
They dress me up, from head to toes,
In lots and lots of rubber clothes.
I wish the sun would come and stay.
I do not like a rainy day.

by William Wise

13

Higglety Pigglety: A Book of Rhymes,
page 13

Getting Ready to Learn

To help children plan their day, tell them that they will—

- listen to a **Big Book**: *I Went Walking*.

- learn the new letters *R* and *r*, and see words that begin with *r*.

- explore animals in the Science Center.

fur/bear   feathers/duck

OBJECTIVES

- Introduce concepts of print.
- Develop story language.
- Reinforce comprehension strategy and comprehension skill.

Big Book

HOUGHTON MIFFLIN
Reading

I Went Walking

WRITTEN BY
Sue Williams

ILLUSTRATED BY
Julie Vivas

Includes:
Science Link

English Language Learners

As you reread, ask children to predict which animal the boy will see next. After reading, have children retell the story as closely as they can remember. Write their sentences on chart paper or have them draw pictures. Children can check the book to compare the sequences of events.

INSTRUCTION

Reading the Big Book

Building Background

Reading for Understanding You remember this book, *I Went Walking.* This time when we read the book, think about whether the animals have fur, feathers, skin, or scales.

COMPREHENSION STRATEGY
Predict/Infer

Student Modeling Review that good readers make predictions about a book, and then check their predictions as they read. What can you predict about the story from the title and the cover picture?

COMPREHENSION SKILL
Inferences: Making Predictions

Student Modeling Who is telling the story? Can I tell from the cover where the story takes place?

Big Book Read Aloud

Reread the story, pausing for these discussion points.

COMPREHENSION SKILL
Sequence of Events

pages 2–9

- What was the first animal the boy saw? What animal did the boy see next?

Concepts of Print

page 11

Capital at Beginning of a Sentence; End Punctuation

What is different about the first letter of the sentence? What do you know about the mark at the end of the sentence?

COMPREHENSION SKILL

Compare and Contrast

pages 16–17

- How is the duck different from the other animals the boy has seen?

 COMPREHENSION SKILL

Sequence of Events

pages 18–19

- What animals have we met so far? What colors are these animals? What animal will we meet next?

Responding

Oral Language: Reader's Theater Have partners act out the story. One child asks, *What did you see?* while the other child answers. If necessary, use the book to prompt children's answers.

 ## Science Center

Materials Blackline Masters 39–40 • nonfiction animal picture books • crayons ....

Prepare copies of **Blackline Masters 39–40**. Children can draw pictures to show animals with fur, feathers, scales, or skin. They may wish to refer to the picture books as they brainstorm animals to fit the different categories.

OBJECTIVES

- Identify words that begin with /r/.
- Identify pictures whose names start with the letter *r*.
- Form the letters *R, r*.

Materials

- **Alphafriend Card** *Reggie Rooster*
- **Letter Cards** *m, r, s*
- **Picture Cards** for *m, r, s*
- **Blackline Master** 174
- **Phonics Center** Theme 2, Week 3, Day 2

Reggie Rooster's Song

(tune: Hush! Little Baby)

Reggie has a rocket that is red.

Reggie keeps it right beside his bed.

Reggie likes to listen to rock 'n roll.

Reggie plays it on his radio.

PHONICS
Initial Consonant *r*

❶ Phonemic Awareness Warm-Up

Beginning Sound Read or sing the lyrics to Reggie Rooster's song and have children echo it line-for-line. Have them listen for the /r/ words and "rub" their stomachs each time they hear one. See Theme Resources page R4 for music and lyrics.

❷ Teach Phonics

Beginning Letter Display the *Reggie Rooster* card, and have children name the letter on the picture. Say: The letter *r* stands for the sound /r/, as in *rooster.* When you see an *r*, remember Reggie Rooster. That will help you remember the sound /r/.

Write *rooster* on the board, underlining the *r*. What is the first letter in the word *rooster? Rooster* starts with /r/, so *r* is the first letter I write for *rooster*.

❸ Guided Practice

Compare and review: *m, s* In a pocket chart, display the **Letter Cards** *r, m,* and *s*. Place the **Picture Cards** in random order. Review the sounds for *r, m,* and *s*. Taking turns, children can name a picture, say the beginning sound, and put the card below the correct letter. Tell children they will sort more pictures in the **Phonics Center** today.

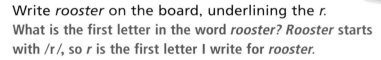

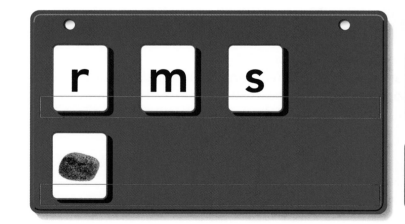

Extra Support/ Intervention

To help children remember the sound for *r*, point out that the letter's name gives a clue to its sound: *r*, /r/.

Penmanship Rhyme: R	Penmanship Rhyme: r
Make a line down, straight and tall. Curve around to the middle. A short line out, that's all!	Little *r* is small. Start in the middle with a short line. Curve at the top, that's all!

Penmanship: Writing _R, r_ Tell children that now they'll learn to write the letters that stand for /r/: capital *R* and small *r*. Write each letter as you recite the penmanship rhyme. Children can chant each rhyme as they "write" the letter in the air.

❹ Apply

Have children complete **Practice Book** page 95 at small group time. For additional penmanship practice assign **Blackline Master** 174. Penmanship practice for the continuous stroke style is available on **Blackline Master** 200.

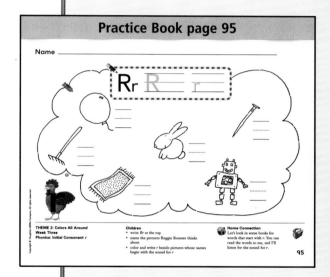

Practice Book page 95

ABC Phonics Center

Materials Phonics Center materials for Theme 2, Week 3, Day 2

Display Day 2 Direction Chart. Children put *Reggie Rooster* (with letter) in one section of Workmat 2. Then they sort remaining pictures by initial letter: *r* and not *r*.

INSTRUCTION

HIGH-FREQUENCY WORDS
Review Words:
I, see

❶ Teach

Review the words *I, see*. Tell children that today they will practice reading and writing two words that they will see often in stories. Say *I* and call on children to use the word in context.

- Write *I* on the board, and have children spell it as you point to the letters. **Spell *I* with me, capital *I*, *I*.**

- Lead children in a chant, clapping on each beat, to help them remember the spelling: **capital *I*, *I*! capital *I*, *I*.**

- Repeat for the word *see*.

Word Wall Have children find the words *I* and *see* on the Word Wall. Remind children to look there when they need to remember how to write the words.

❷ Guided Practice

Build these sentences one at a time. Display the following sentences in a pocket chart. Children take turns reading the sentences aloud. Leave out the pocket chart along with additional **Picture Cards** so that children can practice making and reading sentences.

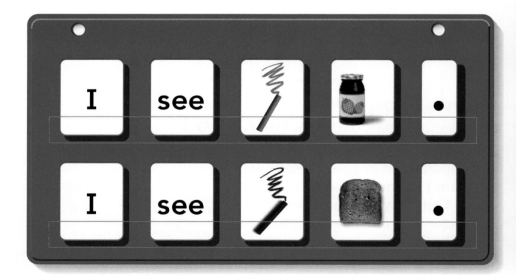

Display *Higglety Pigglety: A Book of Rhymes*, pages 44–45.

- Share the poem "Rhyme" aloud.

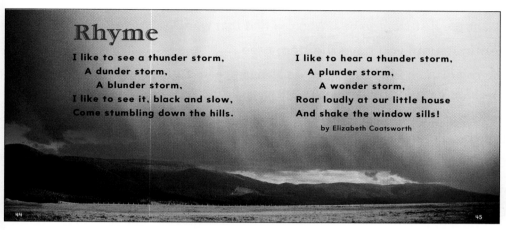

Rhyme

I like to see a thunder storm,
 A dunder storm,
  A blunder storm,
I like to see it, black and slow,
Come stumbling down the hills.

I like to hear a thunder storm,
 A plunder storm,
  A wonder storm,
Roar loudly at our little house
And shake the window sills!

by Elizabeth Coatsworth

Higglety Pigglety: A Book of Rhymes, pages 44–45

- I'll read the poem one more time. This time, listen for the word *I*. If you hear it raise your hand.

- Call on children to point to the word *I* each time it appears in the poem.

- Repeat for the word *see*.

❸ Apply

- Pass out copies of **Practice Book** pages 199–200, *I See* . Read the title aloud. Ask children where they think the father and daughter are going. Point to the daughter and tell children that the girl is telling the story.

- For each page, have children look at the picture and tell what the girl will see. Have them read the page silently. Then ask a child to read the page aloud. Use questions such as the following to prompt discussion:

Pages 1–3 What does the girl see while she is walking?

Pages 2–3 What animals and insects does the girl see? What are the girl and her father getting ready to do?

Page 4 What do you think the ants want?

Then have children count the high-frequency words in the story: How many times can you find the word *I* in this story? the word *see*?

Practice Book pages 199–200

I See

I see [illustration].
I see [illustration].

Theme 2, Week 3, Day 2   1

I see [illustration].
I see [illustration].

2   High-frequency words: I, see

I see [illustration].
I see [illustration].

Theme 2, Week 3, Day 2   3

I see [illustration].
I see [illustration].

4   High-frequency words: I, see

Monitoring Student Progress

If . . .	Then . . .
children have problems reading *I* or *see* in the poem,	have them build the words with magnetic letters and use them in oral sentences.

High-Frequency Words   **T155**

PRACTICE

High-Frequency Words

Tell children that you want them to help build sentences.

- Display the **Word Cards** and **Picture Cards** in random order. Tell children that you will use these words to make your sentence. Review the words together.

- I want the first word to be *I*. Who can find that word?

- Continue until you have the stem *I see* _____.

- The color I want is *blue.* Which card should *I* choose? Have a child place the *blue* card in the pocket chart.

- Place the **Picture Card** *berries* at the end of the sentence. Then read the completed sentence together.

- Continue with other sentences.

Have children write sentences.

- On paper or white boards have children copy the sentence stem *I see*.

- Then have children complete the sentence by drawing a picture of something that is a color they select. Some children may want to refer to the Color Chart to write color words.

VOCABULARY EXPANSION
Using Plural Names

Listening/Speaking/Viewing

Discuss singular and plural nouns.

- Display *I Went Walking*. Page through the book, asking children to name the animals they see. List their responses on chart paper.

- Remind children that some nouns name one person, place, or thing and others name more than one. Read through the list, pointing out that each word names one: *cat, horse, cow, duck, pig,* and *dog.*

Form plural nouns from singular nouns.

- Read through the list a second time. Prompt children to provide the plural for each animal name. The word *cat* names one *cat.* What word names more than one *cat?*

- Write *cats,* explaining how you form the plural. I will add *s* to *cat* to name more than one *cat, cats.*

One	More Than One
cat	cats
horse	horses
cow	cows
duck	ducks
pig	pigs
dog	dogs

Art Center

Materials drawing paper • crayons or markers

Place the chart in the Art Center. Have children draw their favorite animal from *I Went Walking.* Children can refer to the chart to label their pictures.

I yellow dog

OBJECTIVES

- Name singular and plural animal names.

Materials

- Big Book *I Went Walking*

Vocabulary Support

The Vocabulary Reader can be used to develop and reinforce vocabulary related to the instruction for this week.

Vocabulary Reader

HOUGHTON MIFFLIN
Vocabulary Readers
Birds
by Sarah Curran • illustrated by Ande Cook

REACHING ALL LEARNERS
English Language Learners

Display pictures that show several images of the same animal. Say the singular word as you point to one animal; say the plural word as you point to the animals collectively. Have children repeat after you. Listen for correct pronunciation of the plural endings, especially the voiced ending on *pigs* and *dogs.*

Day at a Glance
T158–T167

Learning to Read

Big Book, *T160*

Phonics: Initial Consonant *r*, *T162*

Word Work

Exploring Words, *T166*

Writing & Oral Language

Shared Writing, *T167*

Daily Routines

Sunday	Monday	Tuesday	Wednesday	Thursday	Friday	Saturday
			1	2	3	4
5	6	7	8	9	10	11
12	13	14	15	16	17	18
19	20	21	22	23	24	25
26	27	28	29	30	31	

Calendar

Reading the Calendar Review the days of the week. Count the number of Wednesdays in the month compared to the number of Tuesdays and Thursdays. Write today's date on the board.

Daily Message

Modeled Writing Promote a color when you write the daily message. Today when you help me write, you'll use a (blue) marker. Then we'll see how much you were able to help me. Call on children to write their names or known initial consonants.

Ryan is wearing blue today. Is anyone else wearing blue?

Word Wall

Have children find *I* and *see*, the words they added to the Word Wall in this theme. Then ask them to chant the spellings of the words with you. Call on individuals to use the words in oral sentences.

I	see

Word Cards for these words appear on page R8.

Daily Phonemic Awareness

Beginning Sounds

- Let's play Name That Word. You will listen for beginning sounds. I will say two words, and you will tell me which word begins with Reggie Rooster's sound, /r/. Listen: *rrrope, lllast*.

- Say the words with me: *rrrope, lllast*. Which word begins with /r/? . . . Yes, *rope* begins with /r/.

- Continue with the words shown.

Words in Oral Sentences

- Read "Crackers and Crumbs" on page 7 of **Higglety Pigglety**. Reread a line from the poem: *These are my thumbs*. Clap for each word you hear. How many claps? (four)

- Repeat the sentence, drawing a line on the board for each word. Have children count the lines to verify their answers. Continue with longer sentences.

row/quiet	sing/run
rip/doctor	ball/rain
ring/yes	ten/right
dog/rat	ramp/side

 **Getting Ready to Learn**

To help children plan their day, tell them that they will—

- reread and talk about the **Big Book**: *In the Big Blue Sea*.

- retell a story called "The Parade."

The Parade
by Susan Gorman-Howe
illustrated by Joan Paley

- explore sea animals in the Science Center.

Big Book

HOUGHTON MIFFLIN
Reading

In the Big Blue Sea

by Chyng Feng Sun
Photography by Norbert Wu

Includes:
Science Link

Reading the Big Book

Building Background

Reading for Understanding Display the book and read the title aloud. Mention that the author of this book is Chyng Feng Sun. Remind children that the pictures in this book were taken by Norbert Wu. Tell children that this time when we read the story, they can think of other color words that will describe the fish.

 COMPREHENSION STRATEGY

Summarize

title page

Student Modeling Remind children that good readers think about the important information in a story so that they can talk about it later.

- What do you remember about this story? What kind of information will you look for as we read the story today?

pages 4–7

- What color fish have we read about so far? Were the fish all one color or did they have different colors? Tell more about the fish.

COMPREHENSION SKILL

Inferences: Making Predictions

title page

Student Modeling Let's read the title and look at the picture. What do these tell you about the book?

Big Book Read Aloud

Reread the selection, pausing for these discussion points.

CRITICAL THINKING

Guiding Comprehension

page 1

- **NOTING DETAILS** Where does Norbert Wu take his pictures?

pages 16–17

- **COMPARE AND CONTRAST** How were the children and Norbert Wu like fish? How were they different?

Responding

Oral Language: Summarizing Children take turns sharing information about the fish using picture clues as prompts. Page through the book more than once so all children have a chance to participate.

Practice Book Children will complete **Practice Book** page 96 during small group time.

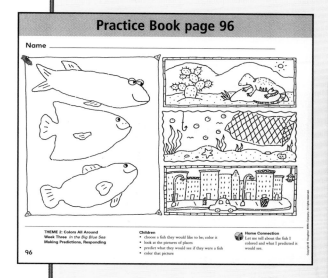

Practice Book page 96

Science Center

Materials nonfiction picture books about the sea • drawing paper • crayons

Place nonfiction picture books about the sea in the Science Center. Have children browse through the books. Then ask them to draw pictures of other animals that live in the sea.

PHONICS
Initial Consonant *r*

❶ Phonemic Awareness Warm-Up

Beginning Sound Read the lyrics to Reggie Rooster's song aloud, and have children clap for each /r/ word.

- Tell children that you will read the song again slowly. This time, if you hear a word that begins with /r/ stand up. If you hear another /r/ word, sit down. We'll do this each time we hear an /r/ word.

- As needed, model standing and sitting alternately for /r/ words as you read the first line. Then reread the song, having children stand and sit for /r/ words.

❷ Teach Phonics

Beginning Letter *r* Display the *Reggie Rooster* card and have children name the letter on the picture.

- Say: What letter stands for the sound /r/, as in *rooster*? Who can help you remember the sound /r/?

- Write *rooster* on the board, underlining the *r*. What is the first letter in the word *rooster*? (r) *Rooster* starts with /r/, so *r* is the first letter I write for *rooster*.

❸ Guided Practice/Apply

- Write *Rr* on the board and circle it. Then write *Rr*, circle it, and draw a line through it to show "not *r*."

- Distribute **Picture Cards** for *r* and assorted other **Picture Cards** to a group of children. In turn, children name a picture, say the beginning sound, and stand below the correct symbol on the board.

- Repeat the activity with different groups of children until each child has a chance to name a picture, say the beginning sound, and stand below the correct symbol on the board.

OBJECTIVES

- Identify words that begin with /r/.
- Identify pictures whose names start with the letter *r*.

Materials

- **Alphafriend Card** *Reggie Rooster*
- **Alphafriend CD** Theme 2
- **Picture Cards** for *r* and assorted others

Reggie Rooster's Song

(tune: Hush! Little Baby)

Reggie has a rocket that is red.

Reggie keeps it right beside his bed.

Reggie likes to listen to rock 'n roll.

Reggie plays it on his radio.

Extra Support/ Intervention

Read "Rainy Day," ***Higglety Pigglety: A Book of Rhymes,*** page 13. Have children "rub" their stomachs each time they hear a word that begins with /r/. Then call on children to point to words that begin with *r* in the rhyme.

Colors All Around

The Parade

by Susan Gorman-Howe
illustrated by Joan Paley

17

PHONICS LIBRARY

Storytelling Practice

Building Background

Let's look at the title page. The title is "The Parade." I see many animals. What are the animals holding? Do you think they are having fun? Help children identify the instruments the animals are playing. (horn, flute, drum, harmonica)

Preview the pictures on pages 18–19. Have children look to see a few of the characters and to predict what the story is about.

OBJECTIVES

- Tell a wordless story.
- Find pictures whose names begin with /r/.

18

19

Oral Language

Go back to page 18. Then page through the story and have children help tell what's happening as they carefully view each picture. Use prompts such as these to help children tell the story:

page 18 **What animal do you see?** (a pig) **What is the pig doing?** (The pig is playing a horn.)

page 19 **Who has joined the parade?** (a duck) **What instrument is he playing?** (a flute)

pages 20–21 **Now who has joined the parade?** (a cow, a frog) **What instruments are they playing?** (a drum, a harmonica)

pages 22–23 **Who else joined the parade?** (an elephant) **Why are all of the animals running away?** (The elephant is using his trunk to make music and the music is too loud.)

Now have children take turns retelling the story page by page.

Phonics Connection

Let's think of some other animals whose names begin with Reggie Rooster's sound, /r-r-r/, that might join the parade. (rabbit, rooster, raccoon, rattlesnake) Point out to children that the animals are running away because the elephant is making such a racket. Explain that a racket is a loud noise. Tell children that the words *running* and *racket* begin with Reggie Rooster's sound, /r-r-r/.

🏠 Home Connection

Children can color the pictures whose names begin with /r/ in the take-home version of "The Parade." After retelling on Day 4, they can take it home to share with family members. (See **Phonics Library Blackline Masters**.)

20

21

22

23

EXPLORING WORDS
Color Words

Discuss colors and patterns of animals.

- Have children recall the colors of fish in *In the Big Blue Sea*. Then display the book.

- Explain to children that often animals are not all one color. Like the birds in *How the Birds Got Their Colors,* animals can have patterns, spots, stripes, and flecks of different colors in them.

- Open *In the Big Blue Sea* to pages 4 and 5. Read aloud the text, and write the word *green* on chart paper.

- Then point to page 4. Is this fish only green or mostly green? What other colors do you see? How would you describe this fish?

- Repeat with the other fish featured in the story.

Use colors to draw a picture of an animal. Have children think about the different colors animals can be. Then ask children to draw a picture of any animal they wish. Tell children to label their drawings by writing the color words that describe the animal. Children can refer to the color words listed on *From Apples to Zebras,* page 29.

OBJECTIVES
- Explore color words.

Materials
- **Big Book** *In the Big Blue Sea*
- **From Apples to Zebras: A Book of ABC's,** page 29

SHARED WRITING
Writing a Graphic Organizer

OBJECTIVES

• Write a graphic organizer.

Materials

• **Big Book** *In the Big Blue Sea*
• **Big Book** *I Went Walking*
• **Read Aloud** *How the Birds Got Their Colors*

Review books and create a chart together.

• Display the list you began in the Exploring Words activity on page T166. Read the words with children, reminding them that these were the colors of the fish in *In the Big Blue Sea*. Write *In the Big Blue Sea* as a column heading. Then page through the book. For each color on the chart, write the word *fish* under the heading.

• Recall with children that they have read about many different animals and their colors. Use the chart as a basis for creating a graphic organizer for the animals and colors children have read about.

• Create a column for *I Went Walking*. Point to the word *green* on the list. Was there a green animal in this book? Who can find it for me? Yes, the duck was green. Write *duck* on the chart.

• Proceed in a similar manner, having children raise their hands when they hear the color of an animal as you reread *How the Birds Got Their Colors*.

	In the Big Blue Sea	I Went Walking	How the Birds Got Their Colors
green	fish	duck	hummingbird
red	fish	cow	cardinal
yellow	fish	dog	goldfinch
orange	fish		
white	fish		
blue	fish		blue jay
purple	fish		
black	fish	cat	
brown		horse	raccoon

Day at a Glance
T168–T175

Learning to Read

Big Book, *T170*
Phonics: Review Initial Consonant *r, T172*

Word Work

Exploring Words, *T174*

Writing & Oral Language

Interactive Writing, *T175*

Daily Routines

Sunday	Monday	Tuesday	Wednesday	Thursday	Friday	Saturday
			1	2	3	4
5	6	7	8	9	10	11
12	13	14	15	16	17	18
19	20	21	22	23	24	25
26	27	28	29	30	31	

Calendar

Reading the Calendar Find today's date on the calendar. Review the month and the day of the week. Then ask children to tell the name of the season, and talk about today's weather.

Daily Message

Modeled Writing Use some words that begin with *r* in today's message, as in the example shown.

Today we will change the rabbit's cage. Reba and Tina will help.

Word Wall

Ask children to find and read the words that they've added to the Word Wall. Call on individuals to point to the words and read them. Have children chant the spellings: capital *I* spells *I; s-e-e* spells *see.*

I	see

Word Cards for these words appear on page R8.

Daily Phonemic Awareness

Beginning Sounds

- Listen as I say two words: *rrring, rrround*. Say the words with me: *rrring, rrround*. Do you hear the same sound at the beginning of each word? . . . Yes, *ring* and *round* begin with the same sound. Help children isolate the beginning sound, /r/.

- Explain that now you will say two words that begin with the same sound. Children should raise their hands when they know the sound. Say the pairs of words shown. For each pair, have children isolate and identify the beginning sound.

ribbon/rocket	tomato/tunnel
night/now	marble/magnet
sister/see	porridge/pond
button/basket	newspaper/number

Words in Oral Sentences

- Remind children that sentences are made up of words. Listen: *My mom is here.* Clap the words as I say the sentence again. How many claps? Repeat the sentence, drawing a tally on the board for each word. Have children count the tally marks to verify their answers. Continue with other sentences.

Getting Ready to Learn

To help children plan their day, tell them that they will—

- reread the Science Links: *What's My Favorite Color?* and *What Do You Do, Norbert Wu?*

- sort words that begin with /r/ in the **Phonics Center**.

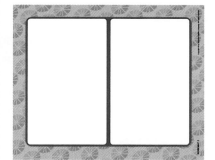

- retell a story called "The Parade."

The Parade
by Susan Gorman-Howe
illustrated by Joan Paley

17

Big Book

What's My Favorite Color?

Reading

I Went Walking

WRITTEN BY
Sue Williams

ILLUSTRATED BY
Julie Vivas

Extra Support/ Intervention

Before rereading the Links, choose pairs of children to revisit the selections by looking at the illustrations and photographs. Children can take turns sharing what they remember about the selections using the pictures as prompts.

INSTRUCTION

READING THE BIG BOOKS
Science Link

Building Background

Reading for Understanding As we read *What's My Favorite Color?*, think about other fruits that are the same colors. Pause for discussion.

COMPREHENSION STRATEGY
Predict/Infer

page 33

Student Modeling Point out to children that the title asks a question. What fruits do you see? What colors are they?

COMPREHENSION SKILL
Inferences: Making Predictions

page 34

Student Modeling Cover page 35 and ask: What do you think the next page will show? (a green fruit; pears) Why do you think that?

Concepts of Print

page 36

Capitalize First Word in Sentence; End Punctuation

- How many sentences are on this page? What can you tell me about the way each sentence begins and ends?

COMPREHENSION SKILL
Sequence of Events

page 36

Student Modeling Cover page 37 and ask: What does the author say first, next, and last? How does what the author says help you predict what fruit will be shown next?

Responding

Oral Language: Personal Response Have children respond to the question, *What color is your favorite fruit?*

READING THE BIG BOOKS
Science Link

Building Background

Reading for Understanding As you read *What Do You Do, Norbert Wu?*, have children think about underwater photographs they might like to take. Pause for discussion.

COMPREHENSION STRATEGY
Summarize

title page

Student Modeling When you tell about this selection, what question should you answer? (the title question)

COMPREHENSION SKILL
Inferences: Making Predictions

page 21

Student Modeling How does the cover help you predict what Norbert Wu does?

Big Book

Science
Link

What Do You Do,
Norbert Wu?

Reading

In the Big Blue Sea

by Chyng Feng Sun
Photography by Norbert Wu

Responding

Oral Language: Literature Circle Have children tell how *What's My Favorite Color?* and *What Do You Do, Norbert Wu?* are alike. Then have them tell how they are different.

Science Center

Materials drawing paper • crayons or markers

Have children draw pictures of different kinds of fruits they have eaten. Have small groups sort the pictures by color.

Challenge

Children can cut out magazine pictures, paste them to pieces of paper, and complete the sentence stem: *I see a _____!* *Click!* to create pages for their own picture books using the language pattern from *What Do You Do, Norbert Wu?*

OBJECTIVES

- Identify words that begin with /r/.
- Identify pictures whose names start with the letter *r*.

Materials

- *From Apples to Zebras: A Book of ABC's,* page 19
- **Alphafriend Cards** *Reggie Rooster, Mimi Mouse, Sammy Seal*
- **Alphafolder** *Reggie Rooster*
- **Letter Cards** *r, m, s*
- **Picture Cards** *man, map, mix, mule, rock, rug, run, sad, seal, six, sun*
- **Phonics Center** Theme 2, Week 3, Day 4

Home Connection

Challenge children to look at home for items or for names that begin with the consonant *r*. Children can draw pictures to show what they have found.

PRACTICE

PHONICS
Review Initial Consonant *r*

Phonemic Awareness: Review Beginning Sound
Display the scene in Reggie Rooster's Alphafolder. One thing I see in Reggie's room is a radio. Say *radio* with me. Does *radio* begin with the same sound as Reggie Rooster, /r/? Call on children to point to and name other items in the scene that begin with /r/.

Review consonant *r* Using self-stick notes, cover the words on page 19 of *From Apples to Zebras: A Book of ABC's.* Then display the page.

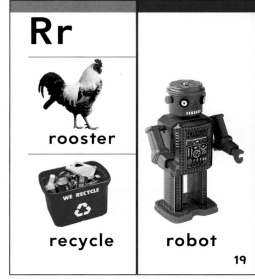

Rr
rooster
recycle
robot
19

From Apples to Zebras: A Book of ABC's, page 19

- Ask children what letter they expect to see at the beginning of each word and why.
- Uncover the words so that children can check their predictions.
- Provide each child with a self-stick note and ask the child to write the letter *r* on it.
- Have children take turns placing the self-stick notes on classroom objects whose names begin with /r/.
- Gather as a group, and list the children's suggestions on the board.

<u>r</u>ug	<u>r</u>adio
<u>r</u>uler	<u>r</u>ecord player
<u>r</u>ace car	<u>r</u>ecorder
<u>r</u>ocket	<u>r</u>ectangle

Practice/Apply In a pocket chart, display the **Alphafriend Cards** and the **Letter Cards** *r, m,* and *s.*

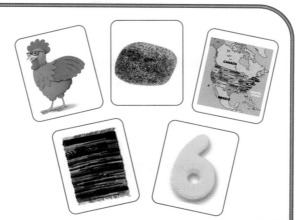

- Review the sounds for /m/ and /s/.

- Hold up **Picture Cards** one at a time.

- Have children name a picture, say the beginning sound, and place the card below the correct letter.

Pictures: *seal, rock, map, rug, six, mule, run, sad, mix, sun, man*

- Tell children they will sort more pictures in the **Phonics Center** today.

- Have children complete **Practice Book** page 97 at small group time.

- In groups today, children can also suggest pictures that begin with initial *r* to add to the **Phonics Library** story "The Parade." See suggestions, page T163–T165.

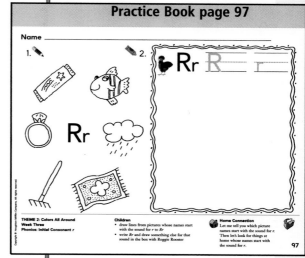

Practice Book page 97

ABC Phonics Center

Materials Phonics Center materials for Theme 2, Week 3, Day 4 ·

Display Day 4 Direction Chart. Children put **Letter Cards** *r, m,* and *s* in separate sections of Workmat 2. Then they sort remaining pictures by initial letters: *r, m,* and *s.*

Monitoring Student Progress

If . . .	Then . . .
children have trouble identifying /r/ words,	have them work with you or a partner to name items in the **Alphafolder** scene.

Phonics T173

OBJECTIVES

- Explore color words.

Materials

- *Higglety Pigglety: A Book of Rhymes,* page 10
- **Picture Cards** *blue, black, green, purple, orange, red*
- **Blackline Master** 41

EXPLORING WORDS
Color Words

Match Picture Cards to color words together.

- Read aloud "I Love Colors" on page 10 of *Higglety Pigglety.*

- Distribute **Picture Cards** to children. Have children match the cards to the words of the poem.

- Tell children that you will reread the poem, but this time you want them to hold their cards up in the air when they hear the colors on their **Picture Cards.**

***Higglety Pigglety: A Book of Rhymes,*
page 10**

- Reread the poem slowly, pausing for children to respond when they hear the color word.

- Repeat with other groups of children.

Draw color word pictures. Place copies of **Blackline Master 41** in the Writing Center. Ask children to draw a picture using the colors mentioned in the poem. Help them to label their drawings.

INTERACTIVE WRITING
Writing a Class Story

Write a class story together.

- Display the graphic organizer from yesterday's Shared Writing activity. (See page T167.) Read through the chart with children.

- Point out that several of the stories you read included different animals that are the same colors, for example, a red fish, a red cow, and a red bird.

- Tell children that they are going to help you write a class story about the different colors and animals that they read about.

- Invite children to share the pen as you write the story. You may want to write the color words in the appropriate color.

We read about a red fish, a red cow, and a red bird.

The red bird is called a Cardinal.

We also read about a yellow fish, a yellow dog, and a yellow bird.

The yellow bird is called a Goldfinch.

Daily Routines

Day at a Glance
T176–T183

Learning to Read

Revisiting the Literature, *T178*

Phonics Review: Initial Consonants *r, m, s, T180*

High Frequency Word Review: *I, see, T181*

Word Work

Exploring Words, *T182*

Writing & Oral Language

Independent Writing, *T183*

Calendar

Reading the Calendar Have children review any words that were added to the calendar this week. Count how many days until upcoming special events.

Sunday	Monday	Tuesday	Wednesday	Thursday	Friday	Saturday
			1	2	3	4
5	6	7	8	9	10	11
12	13	14	15	16	17	18
19	20	21	22	23	24	25
26	27	28	29	30	31	

Daily Message

Modeled Writing Have children help you write the daily message. What kind of letter should I use to begin my sentence? How should I end the sentence, with a period or a question mark?

Today is Annie's birthday. Shall we sing to her?

Happy Birthday

Word Wall

Read the Word Wall together, and then play a rhyming game: Find a word on the list that rhymes with *my* . . . Yes, *I* rhymes with *my*. Find a word on the list that rhymes with *tree* . . . Yes, *see* rhymes with *tree*.

| I | see |

Word Cards for these words appear on **page R8.**

Daily Phonemic Awareness

Beginning Sounds

- Play a guessing game with children. Secretly choose a word, for example, *run*. Say: I am thinking of something you do with your feet. This word begins with /r/. What can you do with your feet that begins with /r/?

- Allow children to guess, correcting them as needed or providing additional clues. Yes, you do walk with your feet, but *walk* doesn't begin with /r/. I'm thinking of something you might do in a race.

- Repeat several times. Then let children take turns thinking of words and clues.

Words in Oral Sentences

- Tell children that you will say some sentences. They'll clap for each word. *I can run and jump.* How many claps? Repeat the sentence, drawing a line on the board for each word. Have children count the lines to verify their answers.

- Here are more sentences: I can skip and hop. I can laugh and sing. Can you play with me?

abc Getting Ready to Learn

To help children plan their day, tell them that they will—

- reread and talk about all the books they've read this week.

- take home a story they can retell.

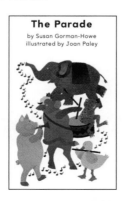

- write in their journals.

REVISITING THE LITERATURE
Literature Discussion

Review the week's selections, using these suggestions.

● Call on children to tell what happened in *How the Birds Got Their Colors*.

● Have children name the animals the boy saw in *I Went Walking*.

● Ask children to tell what animals are featured in *In the Big Blue Sea*. What colors of fish did we read about?

● Preview the photographs in *What Do You Do, Norbert Wu?* Ask if children remember what people with jobs like Norbert Wu's are called.

● For *What's My Favorite Color?* call on children to name the fruits mentioned by color.

● Together, retell "The Parade."

● Children might also recall the Read Aloud stories *I Need a Lunch Box* and *Caps of Many Colors*. Have them tell what they remember about these stories.

● Have children vote for their favorite book, then read the text of the winner aloud.

TARGET SKILL
COMPREHENSION SKILL
Making Predictions

Compare Books Display the books, one at a time, and read the titles aloud.

● Have children briefly tell what each story was about.

● Lead children in a discussion to tell how they used story and picture clues to make predictions about the stories and selections.

ON MY WAY PRACTICE READER
Animal Colors

Preparing to Read

Building Background Read the title. Explain that the boy in this story has just visited the zoo and now he is drawing pictures of the animals he saw there. Draw children's attention to the color illustrations on the front and back covers of the book.

Animal Colors
by Demaris Tyler
illustrated by David Brooks

Houghton Mifflin

Supporting the Reading

Preview the story to prepare children to read independently.

page 1: What is the boy doing? What kinds of toy animals does he have?

page 2: Is it important for the boy to choose the right colors when he draws the animals? Why?

pages 4–5: What is the boy drawing? What color will he make the zebra? What color will he make the moose?

page 8: How do you think the boy feels about his drawings? Which animal was your favorite?

Prompting Strategies

- What is the title of the book? What is the book about?
- What color(s) does the boy need to draw the animal on this page?

Responding

Build Fluency Ask children to guess the answer to this riddle: I'm thinking of an animal whose name begins with /r/. (rooster) Continue with *moose* and *salamander*.

Extend Children can draw a favorite animal, choosing one from the story or one of their own.

Books for Small-Group Reading

The materials listed below provide reading practice for children at different levels.

Vocabulary Reader
Birds

FRUIT

Leveled Reader

Little Big Books

I Went Walking
Sue Williams
Julie Vivas

In the Big Blue Sea

Little Readers for Guided Reading

LITTLE READERS

Houghton Mifflin Classroom Bookshelf

MY FRIEND and I
Sheep in a Jeep
Do Pigs Have Stripes?

OBJECTIVES

- Review initial consonant *r.*
- Review letter names.
- Make sentences with high-frequency words.

Materials

- **Word Cards** *I, see*
- **Picture Cards** for *r, m, s;* choose others for sentence building
- **Punctuation Card** period

PHONICS
Initial Consonants: *r, m, s*

❶ Review

Review identifying initial consonants *r, m, s.* Tell children that they will take turns naming pictures and telling what letter stands for the beginning sound.

- Randomly place four **Picture Cards** along the board ledge. Write *r, m,* and *s* on the board.
- Call on four children to come up and stand in front of a picture. In turn, have each child name the picture, isolate the initial sound, and point to *r, m,* or *s.*
- Have the rest of the class verify that the correct letter has been chosen. Then write the picture name on the board and underline the initial consonant.
- Continue until everyone has a chance to name a picture and point to the consonant that stands for its beginning sound.

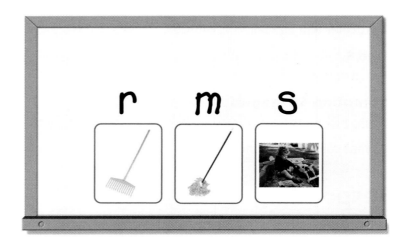

Monitoring Student Progress

If . . .	Then . . .
children need help remembering the sound for consonant *r,*	have them listen to Reggie Rooster's song and listen for *r* words.

HIGH-FREQUENCY WORDS
I, see

❷ Review

Review the high-frequency words *I, see*.

- Give each small group the **Word Cards, Picture Cards,** and **Punctuation Card** needed to make a sentence. Each child holds one card.

- Children stand and arrange themselves to make a sentence for others to read.

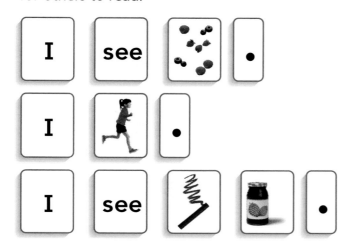

❸ Practice/Apply

- Children can complete **Practice Book** page 98 independently and read it to you during small group time.

- Pass out copies of **Practice Book** pages 201–202, *I See* . Read the title aloud.

- Ask children if this story takes place in a city or a small town. Point to the tall buildings and explain that the class is going on a field trip in a city.

- For each page, have children look at the picture and tell what the characters are seeing. Have them read the page silently. Then ask a child to read the page aloud. Use questions such as the following to prompt discussion:

  Pages 1–3 Where do you think the class is going? What do they see on their way?

  Page 4 Where did they go? What kind of museum is it? What do they see inside the museum?

- Have children count the high-frequency words in the story: How many times can you find the word *I* in this story? the word *see?*

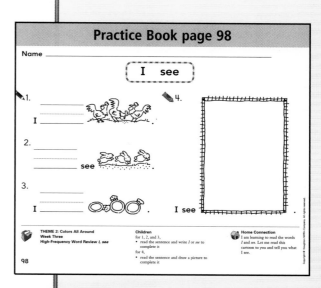

Practice Book page 98

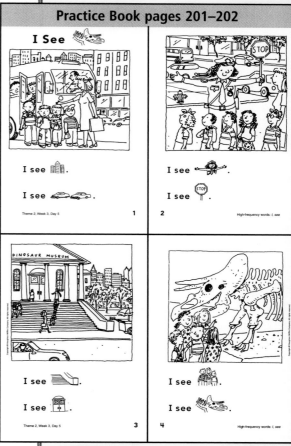

Practice Book pages 201–202

OBJECTIVES

● Explore color words.

Materials

● *From Apples to Zebras: A Book of ABC's,* page 29

EXPLORING WORDS

Color Words

Identify color words.

● Display page 29 of *From Apples to Zebras: A Book of ABC's.*

● Call on children to "read" the color words on the page.

Play an identification game using colors.

● Invite children to play a game of "I Spy" with you.

● Page through the book, choosing a photograph, then display the pages.

● Describe the item you chose, using one or more color words but without naming the item, for example *I spy something red and white.* When most hands are up, have children identify the item.

● As children feel comfortable, have them select a picture in the book and supply the clues to you or to a partner.

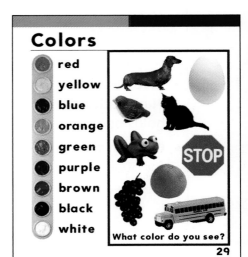

From Apples to Zebras: A Book of ABC's, page 29

INDEPENDENT WRITING
Journals

DAY
5

OBJECTIVES
- Write independently.

Materials
- journals

WRITING

WEEK 3

Preparing to Write

- Review this week's Shared and Interactive Writing posted in the classroom. (See T167 and T175). Point out the naming word chart and the color charts.

- Invite children to discuss some of the things they learned during the theme. Tell them that today they will write about their favorite color activity.

- Pass out the journals.

- This week we learned that some naming words name one person, place, or thing and others name more than one. What new words could you put in your journal?

- We also worked together to make a chart of the colors of things we have read about. We even wrote a class summary. What were some of the colors of things we read about?

Writing Independently

- Have children draw and write about their favorite color activity. Remind them that they can refer to classroom charts, the Word Wall, and the theme books as they write.

- If time permits, allow children to share what they've written with the class.

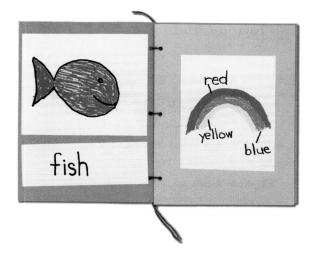

Portfolio Opportunity

Mark journal entries you would like to share with parents. Allow children to indicate their best efforts or favorite works for sharing as well.

Fruit

Summary: *This nonfiction book introduces readers to a variety of fruits, including bananas, oranges, watermelons, strawberries, apples, and pears.*

Story Words

Here *p. 2*

is *p. 2*

the *p. 2*

Building Background and Vocabulary

Explain to children that this book is about different kinds of fruit. Look through the photographs with children. Encourage them to discuss the kinds of fruit they like to eat. Ask them to help you make a list of their favorite fruits.

🍎 Comprehension Skill: Inferences: Making Predictions

Read together the Strategy Focus on the book flap. Remind children to use clues from the title and the cover photograph to predict what they will see in the book. As they read, have children check their predictions.

Responding

Discussing the Book Have children talk about their responses to the book. Ask them to talk about what they liked best about the book. Have children point to sentences or photographs they especially enjoyed. Turn to page 8 and ask volunteers to point out the different kinds of fruits they see in the picture. Ask children which fruits they have tasted and which are their favorites. Have them explain why they like certain fruits best.

Responding Have children answer the questions on the inside back cover. Then help them complete the Writing and Drawing activity. Have children take turns explaining their drawings to the class. Display the pictures on a bulletin board titled *Our Favorite Fruits*.

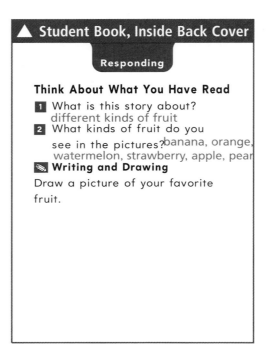

▲ **Student Book, Inside Back Cover**

Responding

Think About What You Have Read

1. What is this story about? different kinds of fruit
2. What kinds of fruit do you see in the pictures? banana, orange, watermelon, strawberry, apple, pear

✏️ **Writing and Drawing**

Draw a picture of your favorite fruit.

Building Fluency

Model Have children follow along as you reread pages 2 and 3 to them. Point out that the first three words, *Here is the,* on the two pages are the same. Tell children that these words begin every page in the book.

Practice Have children work with partners and read the book aloud. For each page, have one partner read the repeating phrase, *Here is the,* while the other child reads the word that tells the fruit seen in the picture. Then ask partners to point out words or pages that they can read comfortably.

Oral Language Development

Color Words Discuss color words with children. Explain that color words are words that tell the color of things. Have children page through the book with you. For each photograph, ask volunteers to name the color of the fruit shown in the picture (*yellow banana, orange orange, red watermelon, red strawberry, green apple, green pear*).

Practice Reread the book with children. Review the color words they used to describe each photograph. Turn to the last page and ask children to name the colors of each of the fruits they see in the picture.

Assessing Student Progress

Monitoring Student Progress

Throughout Theme 2, you monitored student progress by using the following program features: the **Emerging Literacy Survey, Guiding Comprehension** questions, **skill lesson applications,** the **Theme 2 Observation Checklist,** and the **Monitoring Student Progress** boxes.

Your students are now ready for theme assessments, which allow you to assess each student's progress formally.

Testing Options and Multiple Measures

The **Integrated Theme Test** and the **Weekly Skills Tests** are formal group assessments used to evaluate children's performance on theme objectives. Administer the **Weekly Skills Test** at the end of each week. (**Theme Skills Tests** are also available for administration at the end of each theme, beginning with Theme 2.) The first **Integrated Theme Test,** for Themes 1–4, is administered after Theme 4.

In addition, other multiple measures might include: the **Emerging Literacy Survey** (either using previous results or administering again at the conclusion of the theme), the **Theme 2 Observation Checklist,** and **student writing** or **artwork** (both teacher- and student-selected). Multiple measures or assessment can be collected in a portfolio.

Fluency Assessment

Oral reading fluency is a useful measure of a child's development. In the early stages, oral fluency should be observed informally. You can use the **Leveled Reading Passages Assessment Kit** to assess fluency.

Using Assessment to Plan Instruction

Besides the results of theme assessments, you can use the **Theme 2 Observation Checklist** on the next page to determine individual children's needs and determine how to customize instruction of major kindergarten concepts for Theme 3.

Technology

Managing Assessment

The **Learner Profile CD-ROM** lets you record, manage, and report the results of children's progress.

Name _____ Date _____

Observation Checklist

	Beginning	Developing	Proficient
Listening Comprehension/ Oral Language/Vocabulary • Participates in story discussions			
• Listens to a story attentively			
Phonemic Awareness • Identifies beginning sounds			
• Identifies words in oral sentences			
Phonics • Recognizes sounds for *s, m, r*			
Concepts of Print • Recognizes use of capital at the beginning of a sentence			
• Identifies end punctuation			
Reading and Fluency • Tells wordless stories			
Vocabulary: High-Frquency Words • Reads the high-frequency words *I, see*			
Comprehension • Recognizes sequence of events			
• Makes inferences/predictions			
Writing and Language • Writes simple words			
• Participates in shared and interactive writing			

Copy this form for each child. Write notes or checkmarks in the appropriate columns.
The **Observation Checklist** also appears on **Blackline Master 29.**

Resources for Theme 2

Contents

Sammy Seal's Song
(TUNE: YANKEE DOODLE)

Use this music for Sammy Seal's song.

Sam-my Seal will sail the sea when sum-mer is the sea- son.

Sam-my Seal will sail the sea and ne- ver need a rea- son.

Sam-my Seal will sail the sea in ve- ry sun- ny wea- ther.

Sam-my Seal sa- lutes a sea- gull as they sail to- ge- ther!

Sammy Seal's Song
(tune: Yankee Doodle)

Sammy Seal will sail the sea
when summer is the season.

Sammy Seal will sail the sea
and never need a reason.

Sammy Seal will sail the sea
in very sunny weather.

Sammy Seal salutes a seagull
as they sail together!

Mimi Mouse's Song
(TUNE: THIS OLD MAN)

Use this music for Mimi Mouse's song.

Mi- mi Mouse, Mi- mi Mouse, minds her man- ners

in the house. When she sips her milk, she ne- ver makes a mess.

Mud pies ne- ver stain her dress.

Mimi Mouse's Song
(tune: This Old Man)

Mimi Mouse, Mimi Mouse, minds her manners in the house.

When she sips her milk, she never makes a mess.

Mud pies never stain her dress.

Reggie Rooster's Song
(TUNE: HUSH! LITTLE BABY)

Use this music for Reggie Rooster's song.

Gentle lullaby

| Reggie | has | a | ro- | cket | that | is | red. |
| Reggie | likes | to | listen | to | rock | 'n | roll. |

| Reg- | gie | keeps | it | right | be- | side | his | bed. |
| Reg- | gie | plays | it | on | his | ra- | di- | o. |

Reggie Rooster's Song

(tune: Hush! Little Baby)

Reggie has a rocket that is red.

Reggie keeps it right beside his bed.

Reggie likes to listen to rock 'n roll.

Reggie plays it on his radio.

Mary Wore Her Red Dress

THEME RESOURCES

MUSIC

Moderately fast

Texas

Ma- ry wore her red dress,

red dress, red dress,

Ma- ry wore her red dress,

all day long.

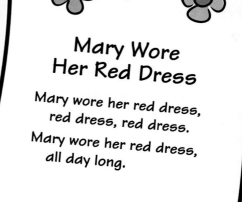

Mary Wore Her Red Dress

Mary wore her red dress,
red dress, red dress.

Mary wore her red dress,
all day long.

WORD LIST

In Themes 1 through 3, the Phonics Library stories are wordless stories to develop oral language. Remaining themes feature the phonics skills and high-frequency words listed here.

THEME 1

Phonics Skills:
none taught in this theme
High-Frequency Words:
none taught in this theme

Phonics Library, Week 1:

We Go to School

wordless story

Phonics Library, Week 2:

See What We Can Do

wordless story

Phonics Library, Week 3:

We Can Make It

wordless story

THEME 2

Phonics Skills:
Initial consonants *s, m, r*
High-Frequency Words: *I, see*

Phonics Library, Week 1:

My Red Boat

wordless story

Phonics Library, Week 2:

Look at Me!

wordless story

Phonics Library, Week 3:

The Parade

wordless story

THEME 3

Phonics Skills:
Initial consonants *t, b, n*
High-Frequency Words: *my, like*

Phonics Library, Week 1:

The Birthday Party

wordless story

Phonics Library, Week 2:

Baby Bear's Family

wordless story

Phonics Library, Week 3:

Cat's Surprise

wordless story

THEME 4

Phonics Skills:
Initial consonants *h, v, c;* words with short *a*
High-Frequency Words: *a, to*

Phonics Library, Week 1:

Nat at Bat

Words with short *a*: *at, bat, hat, Nat, sat*
High-Frequency Words: *my, see*

Phonics Library, Week 2:

A Vat

Words with short *a*: *hat, mat, rat, vat*
High-Frequency Word: *a*

Phonics Library, Week 3:

Cat Sat

Words with short *a*: *bat, cat, hat, mat, sat*
High-Frequency Words: *my, see*

THEME 5

Phonics Skills:
Initial consonants *p, g, f;* words with short *a*
High-Frequency Words: *and, go*

Phonics Library, Week 1:

Nat, Pat, and Nan

Words with short *a*: *Nan, ran, Nat, Pat, sat*
High-Frequency Words: *and, see*

Phonics Library, Week 2:

Go, Cat!

Words with short *a*: *Nan, ran, Van, Cat, Pat, sat*
High-Frequency Word: *go*

Phonics Library, Week 3:

Pat and Nan

Words with short *a*: *fan, Nan, ran, Pat, sat*
High-Frequency Words: *a, and, go*

THEME 6

Phonics Skills:
Initial consonants *l, k, q;* words with short *i*
High-Frequency Words: *is, here*

Phonics Library, Week 1:

Can It Fit?

Words with short *i*: *fit, it, sit*
Words with short *a*: *can, man, van*
High-Frequency Words: *a, go, I, is, my*

Phonics Library, Week 2:

Kit

Words with short *i*: *bit, fit, it, Kit, lit, sit*
Words with short *a*: *can, pan, hat*
High-Frequency Words: *a, here, I*

Phonics Library, Week 3:

Fan

Words with short *i*: *bit, quit*
Words with short *a*: *an, Fan, sat*
High-Frequency Words: *a, here, is*

THEME 7

Phonics Skills:
Initial consonants *d, z;* words with short *i*
High-Frequency Words: *for, have*

Phonics Library, Week 1:

Big Rig

Words with short *i*: *Big, dig, Rig, pit*
Words with short *a*: *can, Dan*
High-Frequency Words: *a, for*

Phonics Library, Week 2:

Tan Van

Words with short *i*: *Pig, Zig, it*

Words with short *a*: *can, Dan, ran, tan, van, Cat, sat*

High-Frequency Words: *a, have, I, is*

Phonics Library, Week 3:

Zig Pig and Dan Cat

Words with short *i*: *dig, Pig, Zig, it*

Words with short *a*: *can, Dan, Cat, sat*

High-Frequency Words: *and, for, have, here, I, is*

THEME 8

Phonics Skills:
Consonant *x*; words with short *o*
High-Frequency Words: *said, the*

Phonics Library, Week 1:

Dot Got a Big Pot

Words with short *o*: *Dot, got, hot, lot, pot*

Words with short *i*: *big, it*

Words with short *a*: *Nan, Nat, sat*

High-Frequency Words: *a, and, I, is, like, said*

Phonics Library, Week 2:

The Big, Big Box

Words with short *o*: *box, Fox, not*

Words with short *i*: *big, bit, fit, hit, it*

Words with short *a*: *can, Dan, Fan, Cat, hat, nat, sat*

High-Frequency Words: *a, is, my, said, the*

Phonics Library, Week 3:

A Pot for Dan Cat

Words with short *o*: *pot, Fox*

Words with short *i*: *big, fit*

Words with short *a*: *can, Dan, Fan, ran, Cat, at*

High-Frequency Words: *a, and, for, I, see, said*

THEME 9

Phonics Skills:
Initial consonants *w, y*; words with short *e*
High-Frequency Words: *play, she*

Phonics Library, Week 1:

Get Set! Play!

Words with short *e*: *get, set, wet*

Words with short *o*: *got, not, Fox*

Words with short *i*: *Pig*

Words with short *a*: *can*

High-Frequency Words: *a, I, play, said*

Phonics Library, Week 2:

Ben

Words with short *e*: *Ben, Hen, men, ten, get, net, pet, vet, yet*

Words with short *o*: *got, not, box, Fox*

Words with short *i*: *it*

Words with short *a*: *can*

High-Frequency Words: *a, I, my, play, said, the*

Phonics Library, Week 3:

Pig Can Get Wet

Words with short *e*: *get, wet*

Words with short *o*: *got, not*

Words with short *i*: *big, Pig, wig, sit*

Words with short *a*: *can, Cat, sat*

High-Frequency Words: *a, my, play, said, she*

THEME 10

Phonics Skills:
Initial consonant *j*; words with short *u*
High-Frequency Words: *are, he*

Phonics Library, Week 1:

Ken and Jen

Words with short *u*: *dug*

Words with short *e*: *Ken, Jen, wet*

Words with short *o*: *hot*

Words with short *i*: *big, dig, it, pit*

High-Frequency Words: *a, and, are, is*

Phonics Library, Week 2:

It Can Fit

Words with short *u*: *but, nut, jug, lug, rug*

Words with short *o*: *box, not*

Words with short *i*: *big, fit, it*

Words with short *a*: *can, tan, van, fat, hat*

High-Frequency Words: *a, he, see, she*

Phonics Library, Week 3:

The Bug Hut

Words with short *u*: *but, Bug, hug, lug, hut*

Words with short *o*: *box, Dot, got, not*

Words with short *i*: *Big, jig*

Words with short *a*: *can, Jan, fat, hat*

High-Frequency Words: *a, here, is, she, the*

Cumulative Word List

By the end of Theme 10, children will have been taught the skills necessary to read the following words.

Words with short a

at, bat, cat, fat, hat, mat, Nat, Pat, rat, sat, vat, an, ban, can, Dan, fan, Jan, man, Nan, pan, ran, tan, van

Words with short i

bit, fit, hit, it, kit, lit, pit, quit, sit, wit, big, dig, fig, jig, pig, rig, wig, zig

Words with short o

cot, dot, got, hot, jot, lot, not, pot, rot, tot, box, fox, ox

Words with short e

bet, get, jet, let, met, net, pet, set, vet, wet, yet, Ben, den, hen, Jen, Ken, men, pen, ten

Words with short u

bug, dug, hug, jug, lug, mug, rug, tug, but, cut, hut, jut, nut, rut

High-Frequency Words

a, and, are, for, go, have, he, here, I, is, like, my, play, said, see, she, the, to

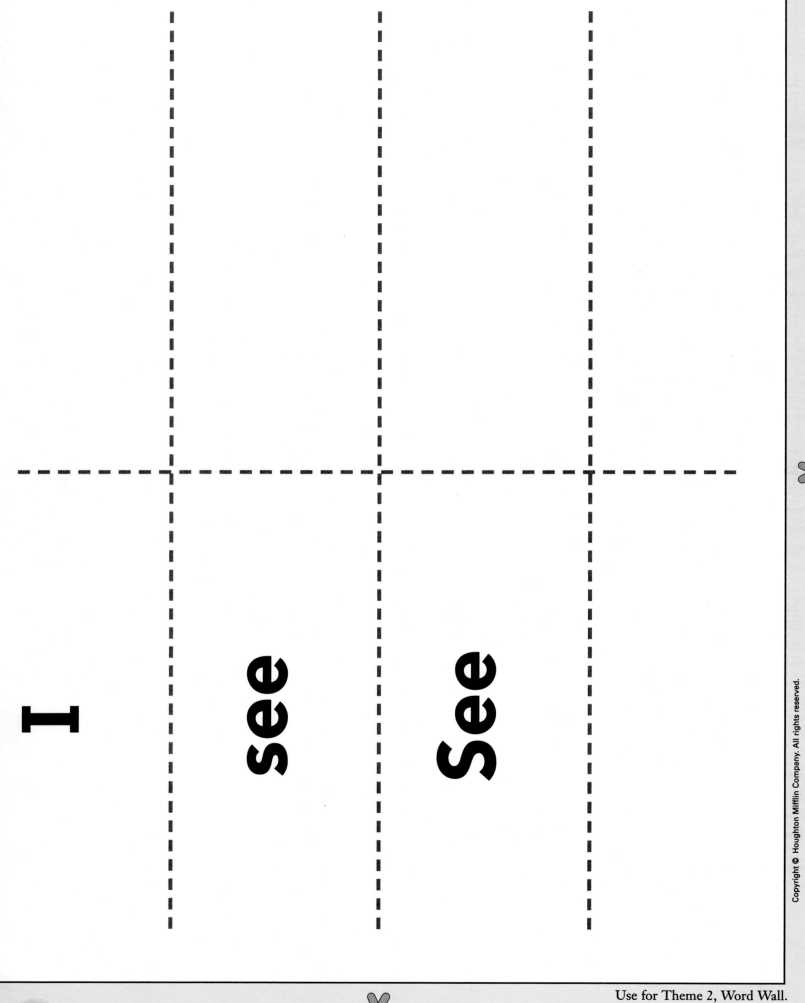

I

see

See

Use for Theme 2, Word Wall.

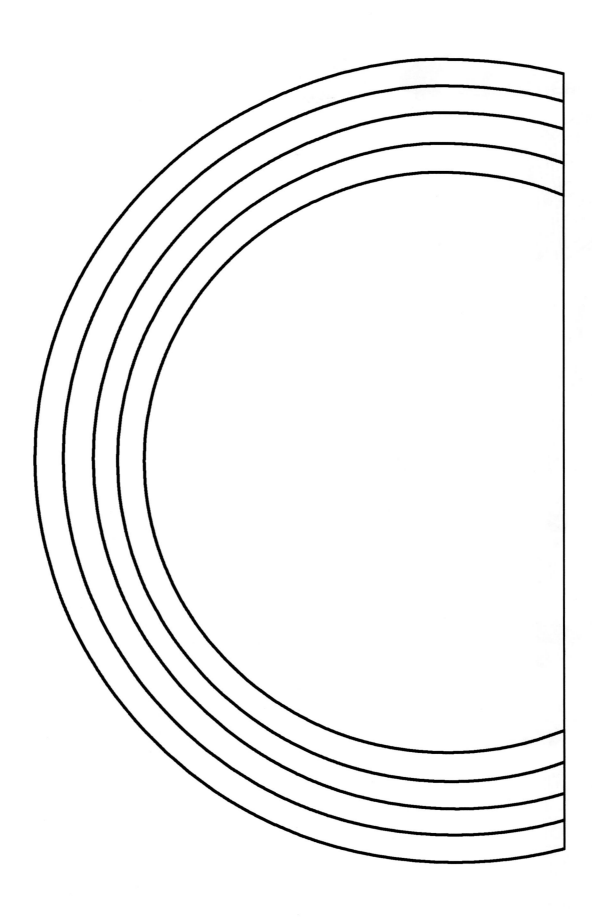

Shape Paper for the Writing Center   Use for Theme 2.

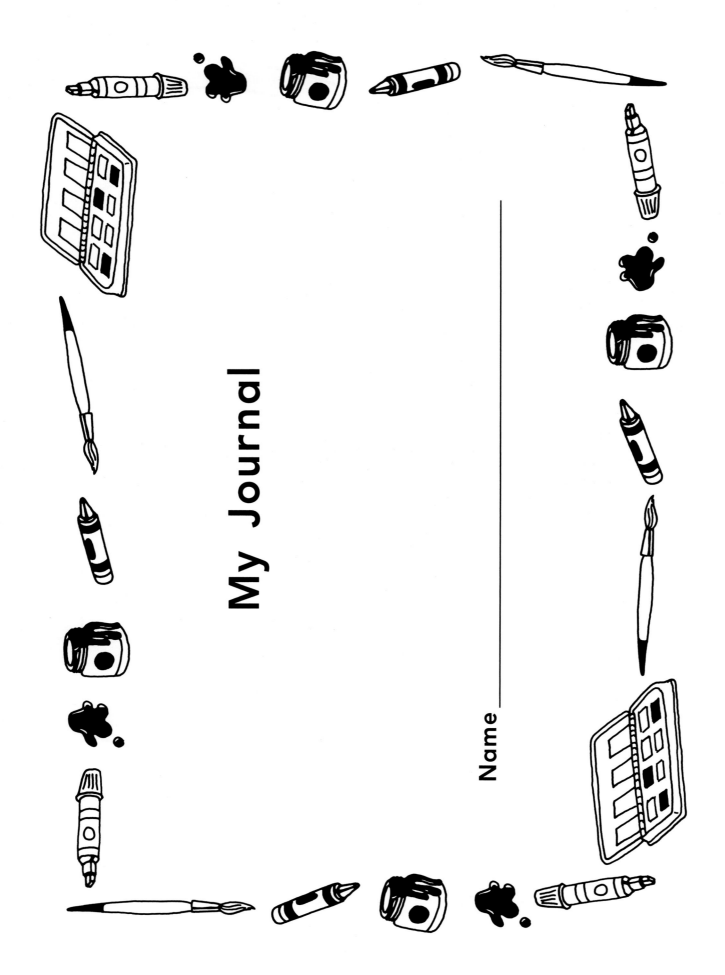

My Journal

Name _____

Use for Theme 2, Weeks 1–3, Day 5.

My Reading Log

I can read

My new words

_____   _____
_ _ _ _ _ _ _ _ _ _ _ _ _   _ _ _ _ _ _ _ _ _ _ _ _ _
_____   _____

Use for Theme 2, Weeks 1–3, Days 2 and 5.

I can follow directions!

Name: _____

Date: _____

Use for Theme 2, Wrap-Up.

TECHNOLOGY RESOURCES

American Melody
P. O. Box 270
Guilford, CT 06437
800-220-5557
www.americanmelody.com

Audio Bookshelf
174 Prescott Hill Road
Northport, ME 04849
800-234-1713
www.audiobookshelf.com

Baker & Taylor
100 Business Center Drive
Pittsburgh, PA 15205
800-775-2600
www.btal.com

BDD Audio/Random House
400 Hohn Road
Westminster, MD 21157
800-733-3000

Big Kids Productions
1606 Dywer Avenue
Austin, TX 78704
800-477-7811
www.bigkidsvideo.com

Books on Tape
P.O. Box 25122
Santa Ana, CA 92799
www.booksontape.com
800-541-5525

Broderbund Company
1 Martha's Way
Hiawatha, IA 52233
800-716-8506
www.broderbund.com

Filmic Archives
The Cinema Center
Botsford, CT 06404
800-366-1920
www.filmicarchives.com

Great White Dog Picture Company
10 Toon Lane
Lee, NH 03824
800-397-7641
www.greatwhitedog.com

HarperAudio
10 E. 53rd Street
New York, NY 10022
800-242-7737
www.harperaudio.com

Houghton Mifflin Company
222 Berkeley Street
Boston, MA 02116
800-225-3362

Informed Democracy
P.O. Box 67
Santa Cruz, CA 95063
800-827-0949

JEF Films
143 Hickory Hill Circle
Osterville, MA 02655
508-428-7198

Kimbo Educational
P. O. Box 477
Long Branch, NJ 07740
800-631-2187
www.kimboed.com

Library Video Co.
P. O. Box 580
Wynnewood, PA 19096
800-843-3620
wwww.libraryvideo.com

Listening Library
P.O. Box 25122
Santa Ana, CA 92799
800-541-5525
www.listeninglibrary.com

Live Oak Media
P. O. Box 652
Pine Plains, NY 12567
800-788-1121
www.liveoakmedia.com

Media Basics
Lighthouse Square
P.O. Box 449
Guilford, CT 06437
800-542-2505
www.mediabasicsvideo.com

Microsoft Corp.
One Microsoft Way
Redmond, WA 98052
800-426-9400
www.microsoft.com

National Geographic School Publishing
P.O. Box 10597
Des Moines, IA 50340
800-368-2728
www.nationalgeographic.com

New Kid Home Video
P.O. Box 10443
Beverly Hills, CA 90213
800-309-2392
www.NewKidhomevideo.com

Puffin Books
345 Hudson Street
New York, NY 10014
800-233-7364

Rainbow Educational Media
4540 Preslyn Drive
Raleigh, NC 27616
800-331-4047
www.rainbowedumedia.com

Recorded Books
270 Skipjack Road
Prince Frederick, MD 20678
800-638-1304
www.recordedbooks.com

Sony Wonder
Dist. by Professional Media Service
19122 S. Vermont Avenue
Gardena, CA 90248
800-223-7672
www.sonywonder.com

Spoken Arts
195 South White Rock Road
Holmes, NY 12531
800-326-4090
www.spokenartsmedia.com

SRA Media
220 E. Danieldale Road
DeSoto, TX 75115
800-843-8855
www.sra4kids.com

Sunburst Technology
1550 Executive Drive
Elgin, IL, 60123
800-321-7511
www.sunburst.com

SVE & Churchill Media
6677 North Northwest Highway
Chicago, IL 60631
800-829-1900
www.svemedia.com

Tom Snyder Productions
80 Coolidge Hill Road
Watertown, MA 02472
800-342-0236
www.tomsnyder.com

Troll Communications
100 Corporate Drive
Mahwah, NJ 07430
800-526-5289
www.troll.com

Weston Woods
143 Main Street
Norwalk, CT 06851-1318
800-243-5020
www.scholastic.com/westonwoods

Index

Boldface page references indicate formal strategy and skill instruction.

Teaching and management
  instructional routines, T9
  management routines, T8
  Managing Flexible Groups T20–T21, T76–T77,
    T132–T135
  setting up centers, T22–T23, T78–T79,
    T136–T137
  special needs of students, meeting. *See*
    Reaching All Learners.

Technology resources, R14

Theme
  Colors All Around, T2–T185

Theme Assessment Wrap-Up, T184–T185

Theme Poem
  "I Love Colors," T15

Theme poster, T14

Theme projects, T10–T11

Theme Skills Overview, T6–T7

Theme, Launching the, T14–T15

Think Aloud. *See* Modeling, teacher.

Vocabulary, extending
  animals, **T41, T157, T166, T167,** T175,
  colors and color names, T26, T30, T39, **T40–T41,**
    T63, T46, T52, T70, T98, T112, T120, T128,
    T166, T167, T174, T175, **T182,** T183
  days of the week, T24, T32, T80, T90, T138,
    T148
  describing words, **T31, T41**
  months of the year, T80, T114, T168
  See also Building Vocabulary Center Activities,
    Language concepts and skills.

Vocabulary Readers
  Birds, T157
  Colors, T41
  Fish Colors, T99

Vocabulary, selection
  high-frequency words. *See* High-frequency
    words.

Word and Picture Books, T51, T97, T105, T155

Word Wall, T9, T38, T32, T56, T64, T71, T80, T88,
T90, T96, T100, T114, T122, T129,T138, T148,
T154, T158, T168, T176

Wordless Books, T51–T53, T109–T111,
T163–T165

Writer's log. *See* Journal.

Writing activities and types
  cooperative writing. *See* Shared writing.
  daily messages, T24, T32, T42, T56, T64, T80,
    T90, T100, T114, T122, T138, T148, T158,
    T168, T176
  descriptions, T63, T113, T121
  diaries, logs, and notebooks, T71, T129, T183
  emergent. *See* Emergent writing.
  independent. *See* Independent writing.
  interactive writing. *See* Interactive writing.
  sentences, T88, T96, T98, T146, T156, T154
  shared writing. *See* Shared writing.

Writing skills
  formats. *See* Writing activities and types.
  prewriting skills
    drawing, **T30, T40, T70, T98, T128, T120,
    T156, T166, T174, T179**